MICROSOFT OFFICE 365 USER GUIDE

A Step-by-Step Handbook for Beginners to Master these Programs for Efficient Workflow

MICHEL M. DUNCAN

DISCLAIMER

The contents of this book are provided for informational and entertainment purposes only. The author and publisher make no representations or warranties with respect to the accuracy, applicability, completeness, or suitability of the contents of this book for any purpose.

The information contained within this book is based on the author's personal experiences, research, and opinions, and it is not intended to substitute for professional advice. Readers are encouraged to consult appropriate professionals in the field regarding their individual situations and circumstances.

The author and publisher shall not be liable for any loss, injury, or damage allegedly arising from any information or suggestions contained within this book. Any reliance you place on such information is strictly at your own risk.

Furthermore, the inclusion of any third-party resources, websites, or references does not imply endorsement or responsibility for the content or services provided by these entities.

Readers are encouraged to use their own discretion and judgment in applying any information or recommendations contained within this book to their own lives and situations.

Thank you for reading and understanding this disclaimer.

TABLE OF CONTENTS

CHAPTER ONE
Introduction

1.1 Overview of Microsoft Office 365

Microsoft Office 365 isn't exactly a new venture, but it's a powerful suite that combines familiar productivity tools with the convenience of cloud storage and collaboration.

Instead of installing software on individual devices, Office 365 allows you to access programs like Word, Excel, and PowerPoint from anywhere with an internet connection. This subscription service also includes cloud-based versions of essential communication and teamwork features:

- Exchange Online: Manage email, calendars, and contacts.

- SharePoint Online: Share files, create team sites, and collaborate on projects.

- Microsoft Teams (formerly Lync Online): Hold instant messaging conversations and conduct online meetings.

Office 365 Versions

Different types of organizations and businesses have varying needs, so Office 365 is available in three versions to cater to end users:

Office 365 for Small Businesses: Designed for small businesses and professionals with minimal IT requirements, this version offers a set of essential tools. It is easy to try (with a free 30-day trial) and affordable ($6 per user per month at the time of publication). It includes Office Web Apps, Microsoft SharePoint Online, Microsoft Exchange Online, and Microsoft Lync for instant messaging and online meetings.

Office 365 for Enterprises: Enterprises have more extensive IT needs compared to small businesses or individuals. This version is equipped to handle a large number of email accounts, messages, and attachments; provide guaranteed uptime; offer comprehensive reporting and support options; and deliver Active Directory features for single sign-on. Office 365 for enterprises includes all these features, extends standard BPOS services, and enhances collaboration and online meeting capabilities. Flexible plans allow businesses of different sizes to tailor the features to meet their specific cloud support requirements.

Office 365 for Education: Educational institutions face unique challenges, such as providing students with access to the latest software on a limited budget. Cloud-based services help educational users save money while giving students the tools they need to create projects, collaborate in real time, and learn to use software in the cloud. This version is tailored to meet the needs of the educational sector.

With Office 365, you get the best of both worlds: familiar applications you know and love, along with the flexibility and scalability of cloud-based services.

1.2 Benefits of Using Office 365

There are several key benefits to using Office 365, including:

- **Accessibility:** Work from anywhere, anytime. Since Office 365 is cloud-based, you can access your files and programs through a web browser on any device with an internet connection. This is ideal for remote workers or teams that need to collaborate on projects regardless of location.

- **Enhanced Collaboration:** Streamlined teamwork. Office 365 applications allow multiple users to work on documents simultaneously. This eliminates the need for emailing back-and-forth versions and reduces the risk of confusion.

- **Improved Security:** Built-in safeguards. Microsoft invests heavily in securing its cloud infrastructure. Office 365 offers features like two-factor authentication and data encryption to help protect your information.

- **Automatic Updates:** Always up-to-date. With Office 365, you never have to worry about manually installing software updates. Microsoft automatically pushes out updates to ensure you have the latest features and security patches.

- **Cost-effective:** Predictable budgeting. Office 365 typically uses a subscription model, which can be more cost-effective than purchasing traditional software licenses, especially for businesses with fluctuating needs.

- **Centralized Management:** Easier IT administration. For businesses, Office 365 simplifies IT management by providing a central location to manage user accounts, applications, and data storage.

1.3 System Requirements and Compatibility

There are two main aspects to consider for using Office 365:

1. **Operating System:** This refers to the software that runs your computer (Windows, Mac, etc.). Microsoft provides different minimum requirements depending on your OS.

2. **Device Capabilities:** While Office 365 can run on many devices, having a computer with sufficient processing power, memory, and storage will give you a smoother experience.

Here's a quick rundown:

- **Operating System:**

  - Windows: Generally, recent versions of Windows (Windows 10, 11) are supported. Even Windows Server versions can be compatible for specific use cases.

  - Mac: Office 365 works on the most recent versions of macOS (typically the last 3 versions).

  - Mobile Devices: There are versions of Office apps available for iOS and Android, though they may have some feature limitations compared to the desktop versions.

- **Device Capabilities:**

  - Processor: A dual-core processor with a speed of 1.6 GHz or faster is recommended for basic use.

  - Memory (RAM): 4 GB of RAM is ideal, though 2 GB is the minimum for Windows (32-bit).

  - Storage: Having 4 GB of free disk space is a good starting point.

  - Display: A screen resolution of 1280x768 is sufficient, but higher resolutions may require additional graphics hardware acceleration.

  - Internet Connection: Since Office 365 is cloud-based, a reliable internet connection is essential.

1.4 Subscription Plans and Pricing

Microsoft 365 (formerly Office 365) offers several subscription plans to cater to different needs and budgets. Here's a breakdown of the key points:

- **Subscription Model:** Office 365 typically uses a subscription model, where you pay a monthly or annual fee to access the applications and services. This can be more cost-effective than purchasing traditional software licenses, especially if you need flexibility or have a growing team.

- **Plan Options:** There are plans for individuals, families, and businesses, each offering different features and user capacities. Here are some popular options:
  - **Microsoft 365 Personal:** Ideal for one person, with access to core applications like Word, Excel, PowerPoint, and Outlook, along with 1 TB of OneDrive cloud storage.
  - **Microsoft 365 Family:** Perfect for families or households, allowing up-to-6 users to share the subscription with the same benefits as Personal, plus additional cloud storage (1 TB per user, totalling 6 TB).
  - **Microsoft 365 Business Plans:** Designed for businesses of various sizes, these plans offer a wider range of features, including cloud storage, email hosting, security tools, and team collaboration features. Popular options include Business Basic, Standard, and Premium.
- **Pricing:** Prices vary depending on the plan you choose and the subscription term (monthly or annual). Generally, annual subscriptions offer a discount compared to monthly billing.

CHAPTER TWO
Getting Started

2.1 Creating an Office 365 Account

Creating a Microsoft 365 account is straightforward. Here's how to do it:

Step 1:

- Go to account.microsoft.com, select **Sign in**, and then choose **Create one!**

- If you prefer to create a new email address, select **Create a Microsoft account**, click **Next**, and follow the on-screen instructions.

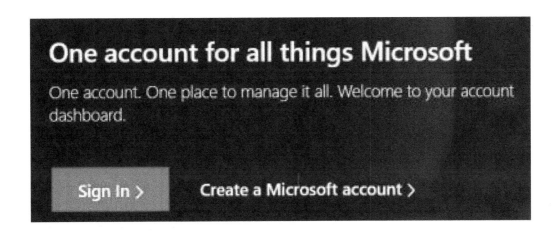

Step 2: Click Create one!

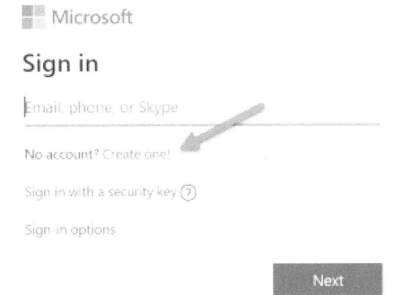

Step 3: Enter an email address you want to create and click Next

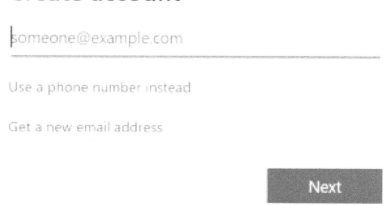

Create account

someone@example.com

Use a phone number instead

Get a new email address

Next

Step 4: Enter a password of your choosing and click Next.

Create a password

Enter the password you would like to use with your account.

Create password

☐ Show password

✔ I would like information, tips, and offers about Microsoft products and services.

Choosing **Next** means that you agree to the Microsoft Services Agreement and privacy and cookies statement.

Next

2.2 Navigating the Office 365 Dashboard

The Office 365 dashboard, now known as the Microsoft 365 admin centre, provides a central hub for managing your subscription and users. Here's a breakdown of navigating the key areas:

Accessing the Dashboard:

1. **Login:** Go to the Microsoft 365 admin and sign in with your administrator account.

Understanding the Layout:

- **Home:** This is the default landing page offering an overview of your subscription, including recent activity, news, and any alerts that require attention.

- **Navigation Pane:** On the left-hand side, you'll find the main navigation pane with sections for core functionalities. Here are some of the most common ones:

  o **Users:** Manage user accounts, add new users, and assign licenses.

  o **Groups:** Create security groups to simplify permission management.

  o **Billing:** View your billing information and manage your subscription plan.

  o **Apps:** Access settings for various Microsoft 365 applications like Exchange Online (email), SharePoint Online (document storage), and Microsoft Teams (collaboration).

  o **Security & compliance:** Implement security measures and configure compliance settings for your organization.

  o **Health:** Monitor the health and performance of your Microsoft 365 services.

  o **Settings:** Manage overall settings for your tenant, such as domain management and directory synchronization.

Using the Dashboard Features:

- **Clicking on a section** in the navigation pane will take you to a dedicated page with more detailed options for that specific area.

- **Many sections will have further subcategories**. For example, the Users section might have options for adding users, managing licenses, and resetting passwords.

- **Look for icons and buttons:** These can provide additional actions or functionalities within each section.

- **Search bar:** There's usually a search bar at the top that allows you to search for specific settings or functionalities within the admin centre.

Additional Tips:

- **Microsoft Documentation:** Microsoft provides extensive documentation for the Microsoft 365 admin centre. Search online for specific features or tasks you need help with.

- **Start with common tasks:** Focus on learning how to perform the tasks you'll need most frequently, such as adding users, assigning licenses, and managing email settings.

- **Explore at your own pace:** The Microsoft 365 admin centre offers a wide range of features. Take your time to explore and learn about the functionalities that are most relevant to your needs.

By understanding the layout and functionalities of the Microsoft 365 admin centre, you can effectively manage your subscription, users, and settings for a smooth and productive experience.

2.3 Installing Office 365 on Various Devices

1. **Visit the Office 365 Portal:**

   - Go to office.com and sign in with your Office 365 account.

2. **Download Office 365:**

   - Once signed in, select Install Office from the homepage.

   - Choose Office 365 apps to begin the download.

3. **Installing on Windows PC:**

   - Open the downloaded setup file.

   - Follow the on-screen instructions to complete the installation.

   - Sign in with your Office 365 account to activate.

4. **Installing on Mac:**

   - Open the downloaded setup file.

   - Drag the Office apps to your Applications folder.

   - Open any Office app and sign in with your Office 365 account to activate.

5. **Installing on iOS (iPhone/iPad):**

- Open the App Store.

- Search for the Office apps (Word, Excel, PowerPoint, Outlook).

- Download and install the apps.

- Open any Office app and sign in with your Office 365 account to activate.

6. **Installing on Android:**

- Open the Google Play Store.

- Search for the Office apps (Word, Excel, PowerPoint, Outlook).

- Download and install the apps.

- Open any Office app and sign in with your Office 365 account to activate.

7. **Installing on Web Browser:**

- Go to office.com

- Sign in with your Office 365 account.

- Access the Office apps directly from your web browser.

8. **Syncing Across Devices:**

- Ensure you are signed in with the same Office 365 account on all devices.

- Your documents and settings will sync automatically across all devices.

By following these steps, you can install and access Office 365 on a variety of devices, ensuring that you have the tools you need wherever you go.

2.4 Setting Up User Profiles and Permissions

Setting up user profiles and permissions in Microsoft 365 involves two main areas:

1. **Adding Users and Assigning Licenses:** This creates user accounts and determines which Microsoft 365 applications and services they can access.

2. **Managing User Roles:** This assigns specific levels of control within those applications and services.

Here's a breakdown of the process for each:

Adding Users and Assigning Licenses:

- **Access the Microsoft 365 admin centre:** You'll need an administrator account to manage users.

- **Add a new user:** Locate the "Users" section and choose "Add user". Fill in the user's details like name, email address, and choose a password reset option.

- **Assign a license:** During user creation, you'll be able to assign a Microsoft 365 subscription plan (license) that determines the applications and services they can access.

Managing User Roles:

- **Access Role assignments:** In the admin centre, navigate to "Roles" and then "Role assignments".

- **Choose the relevant service:** Microsoft 365 offers role-based permissions for various services like Exchange Online (email), SharePoint Online (document storage), and Microsoft Teams (collaboration).

- **Assign roles to users:** Each service has predefined roles with varying permission levels. For example, in Exchange Online, you might assign a "Mailbox User" role for basic email access or an "Administrator" role for managing mailboxes and settings.

- **Add users to roles:** Select the desired role and click "Add users" to assign it to specific user accounts.

Additional Tips:

- **Security best practices:** It's wise to implement the principle of least privilege. Assign only the minimum level of permissions each user needs to perform their tasks effectively.

- **Use Groups for manageability:** As your organization grows, consider creating security groups and assigning roles to groups instead of individual users. This simplifies permission management.

- **Multi-Factor Authentication (MFA):** Enable Multi-factor Authentication for an extra layer of security on user accounts.

CHAPTER THREE
Core Applications

3.1 Microsoft Word

Microsoft Word, a cornerstone of the Microsoft 365 suite, is a powerful word processing application that allows you to create, edit, format, and share professional-looking documents. Here's a glimpse into some of its basic features and functions:

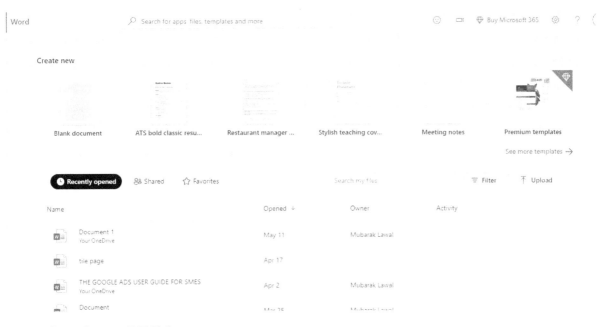

Document Creation and Editing:

- **Create new documents:** Begin with a blank document or utilize pre-designed templates for resumes, letters, reports, and more.

- **Typing and Text Editing:** Compose and modify your text with ease. Utilize features like cut, copy, paste, and undo/redo for seamless editing.

- **Formatting Options:** Change the appearance of your text using font styles, sizes, colours, and formatting options like bold, italics, underline, and highlighting.

- **Paragraph Formatting:** Control paragraph alignment (left, right, centre, justified), indentation, and line spacing for a structured and visually appealing layout.

Formatting and Styles:

- **Font Styles and Themes:** Choose from a variety of fonts to suit the tone and purpose of your document. Apply pre-designed themes for consistent formatting throughout the document.

- **Styles:** Apply pre-defined styles (headings, subheadings, body text) or create your own custom styles to maintain consistent formatting and easily update the entire document with a single click.

16

Collaboration and Sharing:

- **Real-time Collaboration:** Work on documents simultaneously with colleagues within the same document, fostering teamwork and improved efficiency. (Available with Microsoft 365 subscription)

- **Track Changes:** Monitor edits made by others and accept or reject them for revision control.

- **Sharing and Permissions:** Share your documents with others and control their access levels (view only, edit, etc.) to manage collaboration effectively.

Advanced Features:

- **Tables and Charts:** Create and insert tables to organize data and charts to represent information visually.

- **Images and Objects:** Integrate images, shapes, clip art, and other objects to enhance the visual appeal of your documents.

- **Headers and Footers:** Add headers and footers containing page numbers, titles, or other relevant information that appears at the top and bottom of each page.

- **Citations and References:** Manage citations and references within your document using built-in tools (available with advanced versions of Microsoft Word).

- **Mail Merge:** Create personalized mass mailings by merging a data source (like an Excel spreadsheet) with a template document.

Advanced Editing Tools

Microsoft Word offers a variety of advanced editing tools that empower you to create polished, professional, and impactful documents. Here's a dive into some of these functionalities:

Layout and Referencing:

- **Sections and Breaks:** Divide your document into sections with different layouts (columns, headers, footers, etc.) for a structured and organized look. Utilize section breaks for page breaks, column breaks, or next page sections.

- **Tables of Contents and Indexes:** Automatically generate tables of contents and indexes based on headings and keywords within your document, enhancing navigation and searchability.

- **Cross-references:** Create cross-references that link to other parts of your document (like figures, tables, or headings) for easy reference.

Customization and Automation:

- **Macros:** Record a sequence of actions (like formatting steps) as a macro to automate repetitive tasks and save time.

- **Styles and Templates:** Create custom styles for headings, paragraphs, and other elements to ensure consistent formatting throughout your documents. Develop custom templates for frequently used document formats to streamline creation.

- **Building Blocks:** Save frequently used elements like text snippets, tables, or custom objects as building blocks for easy insertion and reuse in future documents.

Collaboration and Review Features:

- **Track Changes (Advanced):** Track changes allow you to see edits, insertions, and deletions made by others. Advanced features let you compare different versions of the document, highlight specific changes, and manage revisions effectively.

- **Comments:** Insert comments to provide feedback or ask questions directly within the document, facilitating communication during collaboration.

- **Content Restriction:** Restrict editing permissions for specific parts of the document to protect sensitive information or control formatting in certain sections.

Advanced Editing and Research Tools:

- **Navigation Pane:** The Navigation Pane provides a quick overview of your document structure, allowing you to easily jump to headings, bookmarks, comments, or specific pages.

- **Research Pane:** Look up information and definitions directly within the Word document without switching applications using the Research Pane. (May require internet connection)

- **Document Properties and Metadata:** View and edit document properties like author name, creation date, and custom metadata for better document organization and searchability.

Exploring Further:

- **Content Controls:** Content controls allow you to define specific areas within your document for users to enter data, such as forms or questionnaires.

- **XML Editing:** For advanced users, Word offers XML editing capabilities to customize document structure and data handling.

- **Document Protection:** Protect your document with passwords or restrict editing permissions to safeguard sensitive information.

Collaboration Features

Microsoft Word offers a robust set of collaboration features that empower you and your colleagues to work on documents together seamlessly, enhancing productivity and communication within your team. Here's a closer look at some of the key functionalities:

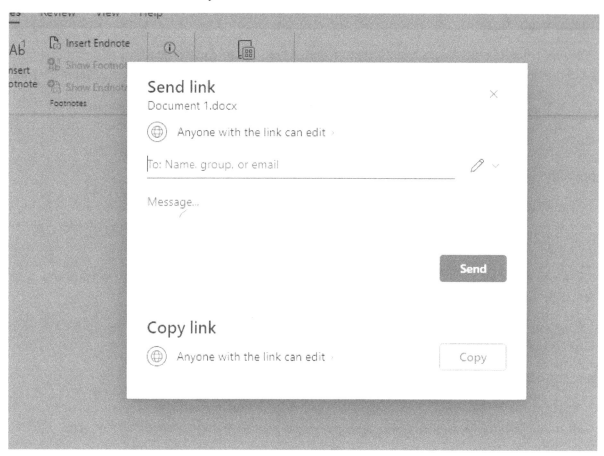

Real-time Co-authoring:

- **Simultaneous Editing:** Multiple users can work on the same Word document simultaneously within Microsoft 365. Edits made by one person are reflected for everyone in real-time, fostering efficient collaboration. (Note: Requires a Microsoft 365 subscription)

- **Distinguish Edits with Coloured Highlighting:** Coloured highlighting identifies which user is making edits in different parts of the document, ensuring clarity and avoiding confusion.

Tracking Changes and Revisions:

- **Track Changes:** Enable track changes to monitor insertions, deletions, and formatting modifications made by others. You can review changes, accept or reject them individually or as a whole, maintaining a clear history of edits.

- **Version History:** Microsoft 365 allows you to access previous versions of your document, enabling you to revert to an earlier version if necessary. (Availability depends on your Microsoft 365 plan)

19

Communication and Feedback:

- **Comments:** Insert comments directly within the document to provide feedback, ask questions, or highlight specific sections for discussion. Replies to comments allow for threaded conversations within the document itself.

- **@Mentions:** Mention specific users with the "@" symbol to notify them and direct their attention to a particular part of the document or comment.

Managing Collaboration:

- **Restrict Editing:** Control editing permissions for specific parts of the document or the entire document. This can be useful for protecting sensitive information or maintaining formatting consistency in certain sections.

- **Share with Different Access Levels:** Grant different access levels (view only, edit, or full control) when sharing your document with others. This allows you to manage collaboration effectively based on individual needs.

Additional Collaboration Features:

- **Co-authoring with Legacy Versions:** Even if collaborators are using older versions of Word (not Microsoft 365), they can still participate in co-authoring sessions with limitations (restrictions on formatting and features).

- **Offline Editing:** With Microsoft 365, you can work on documents offline and your changes will be synchronized automatically once you regain an internet connection.

- **Desktop Notifications:** Receive desktop notifications when someone mentions you or makes a change to a shared document, keeping you informed and engaged in the collaborative process.

Benefits of Using Collaboration Features:

- **Improved Efficiency:** Real-time co-authoring and streamlined communication lead to faster document completion and reduced revision cycles.

- **Enhanced Communication:** Comments, mentions, and co-authoring foster better communication and understanding among team members.

- **Centralized Document Management:** Shared documents stored in OneDrive or SharePoint ensure everyone has access to the latest version and eliminates confusion from having multiple copies.

- **Version Control:** Track changes and revision history provide a clear audit trail and enable reverting to previous versions if necessary.

Templates and Formatting

In Microsoft Word, templates and formatting tools work hand-in-hand to help you create professional and visually appealing documents with ease. Here's a breakdown of their functionalities and how they can benefit you:

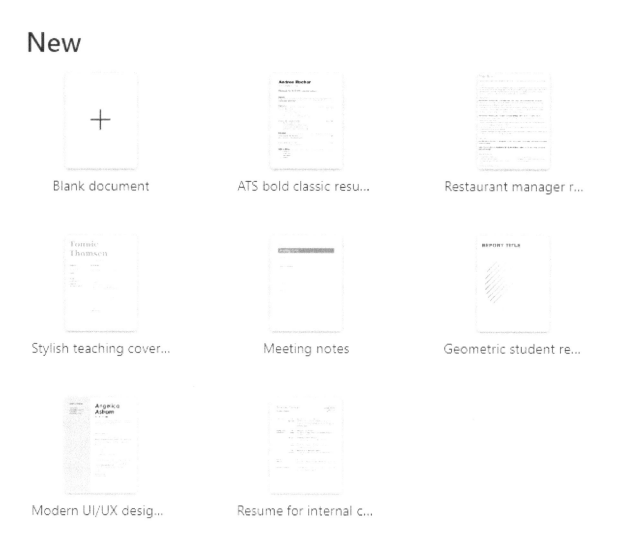

Templates:

- **Pre-designed Layouts:** Microsoft Word offers a wide variety of templates for various purposes, including business letters, resumes, reports, brochures, certificates, and more. These templates provide a strong foundation with pre-defined layouts, styles, and formatting, saving you time and effort in document creation.

- **Customizable Templates:** Templates are not static. You can customize them to fit your specific needs. Change fonts, colours, graphics, and rearrange elements while maintaining the overall structure and style.

- **Creating Custom Templates:** Develop your own custom templates for frequently used document formats. This ensures consistency and streamlines document creation within your organization or for personal projects.

Benefits of Using Templates:

- **Save Time:** Start with a pre-designed template rather than creating a document from scratch, saving valuable time.

- **Professional Look:** Templates offer a professional layout and design elements, ensuring your documents have a polished appearance.

- **Consistency:** Using templates promotes consistency in formatting and style across all your documents.

Formatting Tools:

- **Font Styles and Sizes:** Change the appearance of your text with a variety of fonts, sizes, and colours to enhance readability and visual hierarchy.

- **Paragraph Formatting:** Control paragraph alignment (left, right, centre, justified), indentation, and line spacing to create a structured and balanced layout.

- **Styles:** Apply pre-defined styles (headings, subheadings, body text) or create custom styles to maintain consistent formatting throughout your document. Styles allow you to modify the entire document with a few clicks, saving time and effort.

- **Bullets and Numbering:** Create bulleted or numbered lists for improved readability and organization of information.

- **Tables and Borders:** Insert tables to organize data and charts to represent information visually. You can further customize tables with borders, shading, and formatting options.

- **Sections and Breaks:** Divide your document into sections with different layouts or use section breaks for page breaks, column breaks, or next page sections. This allows for more flexibility in formatting different parts of your document.

Formatting Tips:

- **Theme Selection:** Apply pre-designed themes to ensure consistent colour schemes and font styles throughout your document.

- **Styles Over Direct Formatting:** Utilize styles instead of directly applying formatting to maintain consistency and allow for easy global changes if needed.

- **Alignment and Whitespace:** Pay attention to text alignment, line spacing, and margins to create a balanced and visually appealing document.

By effectively combining templates and formatting tools, you can streamline document creation, establish a professional look and feel, and ensure a clear and organized presentation of your information.

Here are some additional points to consider:

- **Formatting Options:** Explore the Format menu or the ribbon for a wider range of formatting options beyond the basics mentioned above.

- **Alignment with Branding:** If you're working on documents for your organization, ensure the templates and formatting align with your brand guidelines for consistency.

- **Accessibility:** Consider accessibility features like font size and colour contrast to ensure your documents are usable by everyone.

Microsoft Word has established itself as a cornerstone application for creating professional documents. It empowers users from various backgrounds to craft well-structured, visually appealing, and informative content. Beyond its fundamental features like text editing and formatting, Word offers a wealth of advanced functionalities. From real-time collaboration tools to customizable templates and automated features like macros, Word caters to the diverse needs of both individual users and collaborative teams.

Whether you're a student drafting an essay, a business professional creating a report, or a writer embarking on a new project, Microsoft Word equips you with the tools to transform your ideas into polished and impactful documents. As you explore its extensive features and delve deeper into its capabilities, you'll discover a powerful and versatile application that can significantly enhance your writing productivity and document creation experience.

3.2 Microsoft Excel

A spreadsheet is a computer application designed to organize, analyse, and manipulate data in a grid format. It consists of rows and columns that intersect to create cells. Each cell can hold text, numbers, formulas, or even functions. Spreadsheets are widely used for various purposes, including:

- **Personal budgeting and finance tracking**

- **Business accounting and financial analysis**

- **Scientific data analysis and calculations**
- **Project management and task tracking**
- **Inventory management and stock control**
- **Creating charts and graphs to visualize data**

Basic Components of a Spreadsheet:

- **Cells:** The fundamental building block of a spreadsheet. Each cell is identified by a unique cell address, which is a combination of the column letter and row number (e.g., A1, B3, C7).

- **Rows:** Horizontal units of the spreadsheet, labelled with numbers.

- **Columns:** Vertical units of the spreadsheet, labelled with letters.

- **Cell Value:** The content entered into a cell, which can be text, numbers, formulas, or functions.

- **Formula Bar:** Displays the formula or function currently selected in a cell. Formulas allow you to perform calculations based on the values in other cells.

- **Ribbon or Toolbar:** Provides buttons and menus for formatting cells, entering data, using formulas and functions, and creating charts.

Entering and Editing Data:

- Click on a cell to make it active.

- Type your data (text or numbers) into the cell.

- Use the arrow keys to navigate between cells.

- Double-click on a cell to edit its contents.

- To clear the contents of a cell, press Delete or Backspace.

Formatting Cells:

- You can change the appearance of your data by formatting cells. This includes changing the font style, size, and colour, applying borders, and aligning text (left, right, centre).

- Formatting options are typically found in the ribbon or toolbar.

Formulas and Functions:

- Formulas are equations you enter into cells to perform calculations based on the values in other cells.

- Functions are pre-built formulas that perform specific calculations, like SUM (to add a range of cells), AVERAGE (to find the average), or COUNT (to count the number of items in a range).

- Formulas always begin with an equal sign (=).

Creating Charts and Graphs:

- Spreadsheets allow you to visually represent your data using charts and graphs.

- Common chart types include bar charts, line charts, pie charts, and scatter charts.

- You can select a range of data and choose the desired chart type from the ribbon or toolbar.

Saving and Sharing Spreadsheets:

- You can save your spreadsheet file with a specific name for future reference.

- Most spreadsheet applications allow you for different file formats, like the popular .xlsx format used by Microsoft Excel.

- Spreadsheets can be shared with others electronically or by saving them in a cloud storage location.

Popular Spreadsheet Applications:

- Microsoft Excel (part of Microsoft 365)

- Google Sheets (part of Google Workspace)

- LibreOffice Calc (free and open-source alternative)

Formulas and Functions

Formulas and functions are powerful tools that allow you to automate calculations, manipulate data, and gain insights from your information. Here's a closer look at both concepts:

Formulas:

- **Definition:** Formulas are expressions you create within a cell to perform calculations based on the values in other cells. They begin with an equal sign (=) followed by your instruction.

- **Examples:**
    - =A1 + B1: This formula adds the values in cells A1 and B1 and displays the result in the cell where you entered the formula.
    - =A1 * 5: This formula multiplies the value in cell A1 by 5.
    - =A1 - B2: This formula subtracts the value in cell B2 from the value in cell A1.

Functions:

- **Definition:** Functions are pre-defined formulas that perform specific calculations or data manipulations. They offer a convenient way to perform complex calculations without needing to write out the entire formula yourself. Each function typically requires arguments (inputs) within parentheses following the function name.

- **Common Functions:**

- o **SUM:** Calculates the total of a range of cells. (e.g., =SUM(A1:A10)) adds cells A1 through A10.

- o **AVERAGE:** Calculates the average of a range of cells. (e.g., =AVERAGE(B2:B15)) finds the average of cells B2 to B15.

- o **COUNT:** Counts the number of cells containing numerical values in a range. (e.g., =COUNT(C1:C20)) counts the number of values in cells C1 to C20.

- o **MAX:** Returns the highest value in a range of cells. (e.g., =MAX(D3:D27)) finds the largest value from D3 to D27.

- o **MIN:** Returns the lowest value in a range of cells. (e.g., =MIN(E4:E30)) finds the smallest value from E4 to E30.

Benefits of Using Formulas and Functions:

- **Efficiency:** Formulas and functions save you time by automating calculations and data manipulation.

- **Accuracy:** Reduce the risk of errors by using formulas instead of manual calculations.

- **Flexibility:** Formulas can be easily copied and adapted to different parts of your spreadsheet.

- **Data Analysis:** Functions like SUM, AVERAGE, and COUNT help you analyse and summarize large datasets.

- **Advanced Functionality:** More complex formulas can perform intricate calculations and data manipulation not possible with basic arithmetic operators.

Tips for Using Formulas and Functions:

- **Cell Referencing:** Use cell references (like A1, B3) within your formulas to link them to specific data points in your spreadsheet.

- **Function Arguments:** Ensure you enter the correct arguments (values or cell references) when using functions. Refer to help documentation for specific function requirements.

- **Formula Bar:** The formula bar displays the formula currently selected in a cell. This allows you to view and edit the formula directly.

- **AutoSum:** Most spreadsheet applications offer an AutoSum button that helps you quickly create formulas to sum a range of cells.

Data Analysis Tools

Data analysis tools are software programs or online services that help you extract meaningful insights from your data. They equip you with functionalities to organize, clean, analyse, visualize, and interpret data to inform conclusions and guide decision-making. Here's a breakdown of various categories of data analysis tools:

1. Spreadsheets:

- **Suitable for:** Basic data analysis, calculations, and visualization.

- **Examples:** Microsoft Excel, Google Sheets, LibreOffice Calc.

- **Capabilities:** Spreadsheets offer formulas and functions for calculations, data sorting, filtering, and pivot tables for summarization. Basic charting tools allow for data visualization.

- **Limitations:** Spreadsheets can become cumbersome for complex datasets due to limitations in data handling and processing power.

2. Statistical Software:

- **Suitable for:** In-depth statistical analysis, hypothesis testing, and predictive modelling.

- **Examples:** SAS, SPSS, R, Python (with libraries like NumPy, Pandas, Scikit-learn).

- **Capabilities:** Statistical software provides advanced statistical functions, hypothesis testing tools, regression analysis, and the ability to create complex models for data exploration and prediction.

- **Limitations:** Statistical software often requires programming knowledge or a steeper learning curve compared to simpler tools.

3. Data Visualization Tools:

- **Suitable for:** Creating compelling and informative data visualizations.

- **Examples:** Tableau, Power BI, QlikView, Google Data Studio.

- **Capabilities:** Data visualization tools specialize in creating various chart types (bar charts, line charts, pie charts, heat maps, etc.) They allow for easy data exploration, identification of trends and patterns, and clear communication of insights through interactive dashboards and reports.

- **Limitations:** Data visualization tools may not offer extensive data cleaning or manipulation capabilities on their own and often require data to be prepared beforehand using other tools.

4. Business Intelligence (BI) Tools:

- **Suitable for:** Comprehensive data analysis, reporting, and dashboard creation for business users.

- **Examples:** Microsoft Power BI, Tableau, Qlik Sense, Looker.

- **Capabilities:** BI tools offer data integration from various sources, data warehousing, data mining capabilities, and interactive dashboards and reports tailored for business intelligence. They often provide user-friendly interfaces for non-technical users to explore and analyse data.

- **Limitations:** BI tools can be complex to set up and manage, and some may require familiarity with data warehousing concepts.

5. Cloud-based Analytics Tools:

- **Suitable for:** Data analysis on-the-go, collaborative analysis, and scalability for large datasets.

- **Examples:** Amazon Redshift, Google BigQuery, Microsoft Azure Synapse Analytics.

- **Capabilities:** Cloud-based analytics tools offer massive storage capacity and processing power for handling big data. They enable collaboration on data analysis projects and provide tools for data exploration and visualization.

- **Limitations:** Cloud-based analytics tools can incur costs associated with data storage and processing, and they may require some technical expertise for setup and management.

Choosing the Right Tool:

The selection of the most suitable data analysis tool depends on several factors:

- **The size and complexity of your data:** For small datasets, spreadsheets might suffice, while complex datasets may require statistical software or cloud-based solutions.

- **The type of analysis you need to perform:** Basic calculations and visualizations might be handled by spreadsheets or data visualization tools, while advanced statistical analysis would require specialized software.

- **Your technical expertise:** Some tools require programming knowledge or data analysis experience, while others offer user-friendly interfaces for non-technical users.

- **Your budget:** Free and open-source options are available, while some cloud-based solutions or enterprise-grade BI tools may have associated costs.

PivotTables and Charts

PivotTables and PivotCharts are a powerful duo in Microsoft Excel and other spreadsheet applications that work together to analyse and visualize large datasets efficiently. Here's a closer look at their individual functionalities and how they can be used in tandem:

PivotTables:

- **Function:** PivotTables are dynamic tools that summarize and organize data from a source table. They allow you to rearrange, group, and filter your data to identify trends, patterns, and relationships that might not be readily apparent in the raw data set.

- **Key Features:**

  - **Drag and Drop Interface:** PivotTables use a drag-and-drop interface where you select fields from your source table and place them in different areas (Rows, Columns, Values) to control the data summarization and organization.

  - **Filtering and Slicing:** You can filter and slice your PivotTable data to focus on specific subsets and analyse trends within different categories.

  - **Calculations:** PivotTables allow you to perform calculations like SUM, AVERAGE, COUNT, and more, summarizing your data in a meaningful way.

  - **Flexibility:** PivotTables are dynamic— you can easily rearrange fields, change filters, and update the PivotTable to gain different insights from the same data set.

PivotCharts:

- **Function:** PivotCharts are data visualizations automatically generated based on a PivotTable. They translate the summarized data in the PivotTable into a visual format like a bar chart, line chart, pie chart, or other chart types.

- **Benefits:**

  - **Clear Communication of Insights:** PivotCharts present complex data in a visually appealing and easy-to-understand way, making it simpler to identify trends and patterns.

  - **Interactive Exploration:** PivotCharts are often interactive, allowing you to hover over data points to see specific values and drill down into different levels of detail within the PivotTable.

  - **Linked Updates:** Changes made to the underlying PivotTable (filtering, sorting) are automatically reflected in the PivotChart, ensuring consistency between the data and its visualization.

Working Together:

- PivotTables and PivotCharts are designed to work seamlessly together.

- You can create a PivotChart directly from a PivotTable by selecting any cell within the PivotTable and choosing the desired chart type from the Insert Chart menu.

- Any changes you make to the PivotTable, such as filtering or rearranging data, will automatically update in the linked PivotChart.

Benefits of Using PivotTables and PivotCharts:

- **Effortless Data Analysis:** PivotTables simplify complex data analysis by offering a user-friendly way to organize, summarize, and filter large datasets.

- **Enhanced Data Exploration:** PivotCharts provide visual representations of your data, making it easier to spot trends, patterns, and outliers.

- **Improved Communication:** PivotCharts offer a clear and concise way to communicate insights from your data to others, even those unfamiliar with spreadsheets.

- **Flexibility and Interactivity:** The ability to manipulate PivotTables and their linked charts allows for interactive data exploration and deeper understanding of your information.

Excel has established itself as a cornerstone application for data organization, analysis, and visualization. Its versatility empowers users from all walks of life to manage information effectively, perform complex calculations, and gain valuable insights from their data.

Excel's intuitive interface and rich feature set cater to both beginner and advanced users. Basic functionalities like formulas and formatting allow for efficient data entry and manipulation. As you delve deeper, you unlock the power of pivot tables, macros, and data analysis tools, transforming Excel into a sophisticated platform for in-depth analysis and exploration.

Whether you're a student managing grades, a business professional creating financial reports, or a scientist analysing research data, Excel equips you with the tools to transform raw information into meaningful knowledge. Its collaborative features further enhance its utility, allowing teams to work together on spreadsheets and share insights seamlessly.

As you continue exploring Excel's capabilities, remember that it's an ever-evolving tool. New features and functionalities are constantly being added, making it a valuable asset for the long term. By embracing Excel's potential and staying updated with its advancements, you can unlock new possibilities for data exploration, analysis, and communication, ultimately making more informed decisions and achieving greater success in your endeavours.

3.3 Microsoft PowerPoint

PowerPoint is a powerful tool specifically designed for crafting professional and impactful presentations. Here's a breakdown of the key steps involved in creating presentations using PowerPoint:

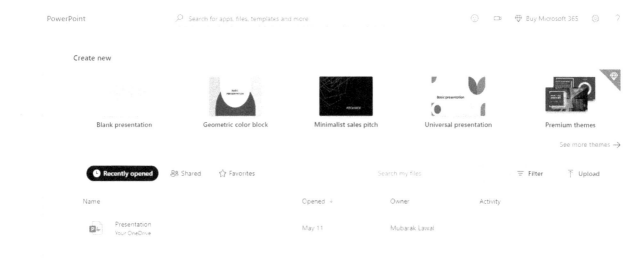

1. Planning and Content Development:

- **Define Your Audience and Goal:** Tailor your content and style to resonate with your specific audience (colleagues, clients, investors) and achieve your desired outcome (inform, persuade, call to action).

- **Develop a Clear Message:** Craft a concise and compelling message you want to convey throughout your presentation.

- **Structure Your Content:** Organize your information logically using a clear flow. A common structure includes:

  - Title Slide: Introduce your topic, presenter(s), and affiliation.

  - Agenda Slide (Optional): Briefly outline the main points you'll cover.

  - Body Slides: Dedicate slides to each key point, using visuals and text effectively.

  - Conclusion Slide: Summarize your main points and reiterate your call to action.

2. Building Your Slides:

- **Start with a Template:** PowerPoint offers a variety of pre-designed templates to jumpstart your presentation with a professional look. You can customize these templates with your branding or choose a blank template for more control.

- **Layouts and Content Placeholders:** Each slide layout provides content placeholders for text, images, charts, and other elements.

- **Adding Text and Content:** Fill the placeholders with your concise and impactful content. Use bullet points and short phrases for better readability.

- **Formatting for Impact:** Utilize the formatting options to ensure clarity. Choose easy-to-read fonts, consistent font sizes and colours, and apply alignment for a balanced look.

3. Visuals and Multimedia:

- **Incorporate Images and Graphics:** Use high-quality images, icons, and infographics to enhance understanding and visual appeal. Ensure visuals are relevant and complement your content.

- **Charts and Graphs:** Leverage charts and graphs to represent data effectively. Let visuals do the talking for complex information.

- **Multimedia Integration:** (Optional) If appropriate, embed videos or audio clips to add dynamism and further engage your audience.

4. Transitions and Animations:

- **Transitions:** Use subtle slide transitions to create a smooth flow between slides. Avoid excessive or distracting animations.

- **Animations:** Emphasize key points with subtle animations on text or graphics. Use animations sparingly to maintain focus on your content.

5. Adding Polish:

- **Proofread and Edit:** Carefully proofread your slides for typos and grammatical errors. Ensure clarity and conciseness in your wording.

- **Speaker Notes:** Add speaker notes below each slide to guide your delivery and provide additional information not included on the slides themselves.

- **Review and Revise:** Take time to review your presentation as a whole. Refine the flow, adjust pacing, and ensure a clear and cohesive message.

Presenting with Confidence:

- **Practice Your Delivery:** Rehearse your presentation out loud to refine your timing, pace, and flow.

- **Project Confidence:** Maintain eye contact, use natural gestures, and project confidence through your voice and body language.

- **Engage Your Audience:** Invite questions throughout or after your presentation to keep your audience engaged.

- **Be Prepared for Technical Difficulties:** Have a backup plan in case of technical issues. Consider exporting your presentation to a different format or printing handouts for your audience.

Design and Layout

Design and layout are fundamental aspects of various creative fields, influencing how information is presented and visually perceived. Both work together to establish a visually appealing and functional structure for any project, be it a physical product, a website, or a printed document.

Design:

- **Focuses on the overall visual concept:** Design encompasses the visual elements that give form and meaning to your project. This includes:

  - **Selection of visual elements:** Choosing appropriate colours, fonts, images, icons, and other visual components that create a cohesive aesthetic.

  - **Hierarchy and balance:** Arranging elements in a way that guides the viewer's attention and establishes a sense of order and balance.

  - **Brand identity (if applicable):** Aligning the visual elements with brand guidelines to create consistency and recognition.

Layout:

- **Focuses on the arrangement of elements:** Layout refers to the specific placement and organization of visual elements within a given space. This includes:

- ○ **Whitespace:** Using negative space effectively to create balance and avoid clutter.
- ○ **Alignment and proximity:** Positioning elements strategically to create visual connections and relationships.
- ○ **Grid systems (optional):** Utilizing grids to structure your layout and ensure consistency and alignment.

Why Design and Layout Are Important:

- **Clarity and Communication:** Effective design and layout guide the viewer's eye, making your message clear and easy to understand.
- **Visual Appeal:** An attractive presentation grabs attention, keeps viewers engaged, and leaves a positive impression.
- **Functionality:** A well-organized layout ensures users can find information or complete tasks intuitively.
- **Brand Identity:** Consistent design and layout reinforce brand recognition and create a professional image.

Principles of Design and Layout:

- **Balance:** Arranging elements to create a sense of visual equilibrium.
- **Contrast:** Using differences in colour, size, or value to create visual interest and hierarchy.
- **Hierarchy:** Establishing a clear order of importance for elements, guiding the viewer's attention.
- **Emphasis:** Drawing attention to specific elements using techniques like contrast or isolation.
- **Proportion:** Creating a sense of visual harmony between elements of different sizes.
- **Rhythm and Repetition:** Using recurring elements or patterns to create a sense of flow and unity.

Design and Layout in Different Fields:

- **Graphic Design:** Creating visually appealing and informative products like posters, brochures, and logos.
- **Web Design:** Structuring and designing websites for usability and aesthetics.
- **User Interface (UI) Design:** Crafting user interfaces for software and applications to ensure a smooth user experience.
- **Product Design:** Shaping the physical form and user interaction of a product.
- **Typography:** Choosing and arranging fonts to create visually appealing and readable text.

Multimedia Integration

Multimedia integration refers to the strategic combining of different media types within a single presentation, project, or learning experience. It goes beyond simply adding pictures or videos. The goal is to create a richer, more engaging, and impactful experience for the audience by leveraging the strengths of various media formats.

Here's a breakdown of the benefits and considerations for multimedia integration:

Benefits:

- **Enhanced Engagement:** Multimedia presentations are more captivating than traditional text-based formats. The use of visuals, audio, and interactivity keeps the audience's attention and fosters deeper understanding.

- **Improved Communication:** Complex information can be conveyed more effectively through multimedia. Visuals can simplify data analysis, and audio narration can add clarity and context.

- **Accessibility:** Multimedia caters to different learning styles. Visual learners benefit from images and videos, while auditory learners gain from audio narration. Interactive elements can engage kinesthetic learners.

- **Increased Emotional Impact:** Multimedia can evoke emotions and create a lasting impression on the audience. Music, sound effects, and visuals can set the mood and connect with viewers on a deeper level.

- **Interactivity:** Multimedia allows for interactive experiences, encouraging audience participation and promoting active learning. This can be through quizzes, polls, simulations, or branching narratives.

Considerations for Effective Multimedia Integration:

- **Relevance and Purpose:** Every media element should be relevant to your message and contribute to your overall objective. Avoid using multimedia for mere decoration.

- **Quality Matters:** Use high-quality visuals, audio, and video clips. Grainy images, distorted sound, or blurry videos can detract from your presentation.

- **Technical Considerations:** Ensure your chosen media formats are compatible with the platform you'll be using for presentation or delivery. Test everything beforehand to avoid technical glitches.

- **Accessibility for All:** Consider incorporating closed captions for videos, transcripts for audio content, and alternative text descriptions for images to ensure accessibility for viewers with disabilities.

- **Balance is Key:** Don't overload your presentation with too many multimedia elements. Strive for a balanced approach that complements your content without overwhelming the audience.

Examples of Multimedia Integration:

- **Presentations:** Incorporate images, infographics, charts, videos, and audio clips to enhance your PowerPoint or Google Slides presentations.

- **E-Learning Courses:** Combine text, audio narration, animations, interactive quizzes, and video demonstrations to create engaging learning experiences.

- **Websites:** Integrate multimedia elements like product videos, customer testimonials, interactive maps, and audio samples to create a dynamic and informative website.

- **Museums and Exhibits:** Use multimedia installations with touchscreens, audio guides, and interactive displays to bring exhibits to life and engage visitors.

Sharing and Presenting

Sharing and presenting go hand-in-hand, and the approach you take will depend on the format of your content and the size of your audience. Here's a breakdown of different methods for sharing and presenting your work:

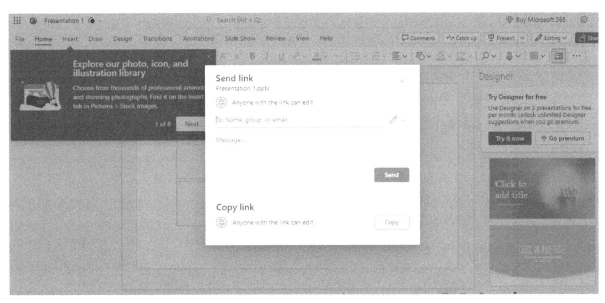

Sharing Documents and Spreadsheets:

- **File Sharing Services:** Popular options include Google Drive, Dropbox, and Microsoft OneDrive. These platforms allow you to upload your files (documents, spreadsheets, presentations) and share them with others via a link or email invitation. You can control access levels, allowing recipients to view, edit, or comment on your work.

- **Email Attachments:** You can directly attach your documents or spreadsheets to emails and send them to specific recipients. This method is suitable for small file sizes and limited audiences.

Sharing Presentations:

- **Presentation Software Features:** Both PowerPoint and Google Slides offer built-in features for sharing presentations. You can present remotely via a link or embed the presentation within a website. Some features allow real-time collaboration and audience interaction.

- **Screen Sharing Platforms:** Tools like Zoom, Microsoft Teams, and Google Meet enable screen sharing while on a video call. This allows you to present your slides in real-time along with audio narration and audience interaction.

General Tips for Effective Sharing and Presenting:

- **Know Your Audience:** Tailor your presentation style and content to resonate with your specific audience.

- **Prepare Well:** Rehearse your delivery beforehand to ensure smooth flow and confident presentation.

- **Visual Appeal:** Use clear visuals, well-formatted slides, and high-quality multimedia elements to keep your audience engaged.

- **Clear Communication:** Structure your content logically, speak clearly and concisely, and avoid jargon or overly technical language.

- **Engage Your Audience:** Maintain eye contact, use body language effectively, and incorporate interactive elements (polls, Q&A) to keep your audience attentive.

- **Practice Active Listening:** During Q&A sessions, listen attentively to questions and address them clearly and concisely.

Microsoft PowerPoint has established itself as the go-to application for crafting impactful presentations. Its intuitive interface and comprehensive feature set empower users of all experience levels to create visually compelling and informative content.

PowerPoint goes beyond static slides. It allows you to integrate multimedia elements like charts, graphs, images, videos, and even audio for a truly engaging experience. Presenter tools further enhance delivery by providing features for speaker notes, smooth slide transitions, and audience interaction.

Whether you're a student presenting a project, a business professional delivering a proposal, or a trainer conducting a workshop, PowerPoint equips you with the tools to effectively communicate your message and capture your audience's attention. Its versatility makes it a valuable asset in various fields, from education and marketing to sales and entrepreneurship.

As PowerPoint continues to evolve, with new features and functionalities constantly being added, it remains a powerful tool for the modern presenter. By harnessing its potential and staying updated with its advancements, you can transform your presentations into memorable experiences that drive understanding, inspire action, and achieve your desired outcomes.

3.4 Microsoft Outlook

Microsoft Outlook offers a robust suite of features to conquer your inbox and streamline your email workflow. Here's a breakdown of key strategies to achieve email management mastery:

Organization and Navigation:

- **Folders and Subfolders:** Create a filing system using folders and subfolders to categorize emails by project, client, or topic. This keeps your inbox organized and emails easily retrievable.

- **Search Function:** Utilize Outlook's powerful search functionality to quickly find specific emails using keywords, dates, senders, or recipients.

Prioritization and Automation:

- **Importance Flag and Tags:** Mark important emails with the "Important" flag and categorize them with relevant tags for better prioritization. Leverage color-coding to visually distinguish important messages.

- **Rules and Automation:** Set up automated rules to filter emails based on specific criteria (sender, subject line, keywords) and move them to designated folders or delete them. This helps declutter your inbox and saves time managing routine emails.

Staying Focused:

- **Inbox Views:** Utilize the various inbox views like "Unread," "Flagged," or "Categorized" to focus on specific sets of emails and avoid distractions.

- **Reading Pane:** Enable the reading pane to preview emails without opening them entirely, allowing you to quickly scan and prioritize your messages.

Improving Communication:

- **Templates:** Create email templates for commonly used responses to save time and ensure consistent messaging.

- **Signatures:** Include a professional email signature with your contact information and relevant links in every outgoing email.

Collaboration and Delegation:

- **To-Do Lists and Tasks:** Integrate Outlook's to-do list functionality to convert actionable emails into tasks and track your progress. You can even assign tasks to others within your organization.

- **Shared Mailboxes and Calendars:** Set up shared mailboxes for teams to collaborate on projects and manage group inboxes. Shared calendars allow teams to schedule meetings and track everyone's availability.

Calendar and Scheduling

Microsoft Outlook offers a powerful calendar and scheduling system, allowing you to efficiently manage your appointments, meetings, and tasks. Here's a breakdown of key functionalities to optimize your scheduling:

Creating Appointments and Events:

- **Detailed Entries:** Schedule appointments with specific dates, times, durations, and locations. Include detailed descriptions and attachments for reference.

- **Invitees and Recurrence:** Add attendees (internal/external) to your events and set recurring meetings for regular events (weekly staff meetings, monthly check-ins).

- **Availability Checking:** Outlook automatically checks invitees' availability based on their calendars, suggesting suitable times for meetings and reducing scheduling conflicts.

Managing Your Schedule:

- **Multiple Calendar Views:** Choose between daily, weekly, workweek, or monthly view to visualize your schedule effectively and identify gaps for new appointments.

- **Colour Coding and Categorization:** Assign colours to different categories (meetings, personal appointments, deadlines) for a clear visual representation of your schedule's composition.

- **Free/Busy Sharing:** Share your availability with colleagues or clients, allowing them to easily schedule meetings with you based on your free time slots.

Collaboration and Team Scheduling:

- **Shared Calendars:** Create shared calendars for teams to track project deadlines, team events, and individual schedules within a project, fostering transparency and collaboration.

- **Meeting Booking Tools:** Integrate Outlook with online scheduling tools like Calendly or Doodle to allow external attendees to easily book appointments with you based on your available time slots.

- **Meeting Requests and Responses:** Send meeting requests with clear agendas and manage RSVPs from invitees, keeping track of confirmations and potential conflicts.

Contacts and Address Book

Microsoft Outlook provides a comprehensive contacts management system, the Address Book, to streamline how you store, organize, and access information about the people you interact with. Here's a closer look at its functionalities and how to leverage them for efficient contact management:

Creating and Managing Contacts:

- **Detailed Contact Profiles:** Create individual contact entries with comprehensive information, including names, email addresses, phone numbers, mailing addresses, company affiliations, and even notes or attachments.

- **Multiple Contact Folders:** Organize your contacts with a hierarchical folder structure. Create folders for different categories (clients, colleagues, family, friends) for easier searching and retrieval.

- **Import and Export:** Import contacts from various sources (CSV files, social media) and export them when needed to maintain data flexibility.

Utilizing the Address Book:

- **Centralized Contact Repository:** The Address Book functions as a central hub for all your contacts, offering a unified view across different folders.

- **Search and Find:** Utilize the search bar to quickly find specific contacts by name, email address, or any other information stored in their profiles.

- **Adding Contacts from Emails:** When you receive an email from someone new, you can easily add them as a contact directly from the email with a few clicks, saving time and effort.

Additional Features:

- **Contact Groups:** Create contact groups to simplify communication with a collection of people. Send emails or schedule meetings with the entire group simultaneously.

- **Distribution Lists (DLs):** (For organizations with Exchange Server) Create and manage distribution lists for internal communication. DLs function as email aliases, allowing you to send messages to a group of colleagues using a single address.

- **Linking Contacts:** Link related contacts (e.g., colleagues within the same company) for easier information access and relationship visualization.

Benefits of Effective Contact Management:

- **Improved Communication Efficiency:** Having a well-organized address book allows you to quickly find contact information and streamline communication efforts.

- **Reduced Errors:** Accurate and centralized contact information minimizes the risk of typos or outdated information in your emails.

- **Enhanced Network Management:** Categorizing contacts by groups or projects facilitates targeted communication and relationship building within your network.

Tips for Effective Contact Management:

- **Regular Review and Update:** Periodically review your contacts and update information to ensure accuracy and avoid sending emails to outdated addresses.

- **Add Notes and Reminders:** Utilize the notes section in contact profiles to store additional information or set reminders for following up with specific contacts.

- **Leverage Contact Groups and DLs:** Take advantage of groups and DLs to simplify communication with frequently contacted individuals or teams.

Task Management

Microsoft Outlook offers a built-in task management system, alongside integration with the separate Microsoft To Do app, to help you stay organized and on top of your deadlines. Here's a breakdown of how to leverage these functionalities for effective task management:

Using Tasks in Outlook:

- **Creating Tasks:** Add tasks directly from the Tasks section or by converting emails into actionable items with due dates and priorities.

- **Prioritization and Categorization:** Mark tasks as "important" and assign categories (work, personal) to prioritize your workload and visually differentiate between tasks.

- **Setting Reminders and Tracking Progress:** Set reminders for deadlines and track your progress as you complete tasks, ensuring you stay on top of your commitments.

- **Flag and Filter:** Flag critical tasks for easy identification and utilize filters to view specific task categories or due dates, allowing you to focus on what matters most.

Microsoft To Do Integration:

- **Enhanced Interface:** Microsoft To Do offers a modern and user-friendly interface specifically designed for task management.

- **Cross-Platform Accessibility:** Access your tasks from any device (desktop, phone, web) with the To Do app, ensuring seamless task management on the go.

- **Smart Lists and Suggestions:** Utilize smart lists like "Today" or "Important" to prioritize your tasks, and leverage To Do's suggestions to help you stay focused and productive.

Additional Tips for Effective Task Management:

- **Break Down Large Tasks:** Divide complex projects into smaller, more manageable sub-tasks to feel less overwhelmed and track progress more effectively.

- **Set Realistic Deadlines:** Be realistic when setting deadlines for tasks to avoid overcommitting yourself and ensure timely completion.

- **Schedule Time for Tasks:** Block out dedicated time slots in your calendar to focus on specific tasks, promoting focused work and preventing distractions.

- **Review and Update Regularly:** Regularly review your task list, adjust priorities as needed, and update task statuses to maintain an accurate representation of your workflow.

Choosing Between Outlook Tasks and To Do:

- **Simple Task Management:** For basic to-do lists and task management within Outlook, the built-in Tasks function might suffice.

- **Advanced Features and Integration:** If you require a more feature-rich experience, cross-platform accessibility, and smart list functionalities, consider using the dedicated Microsoft To Do app.

3.5 Microsoft OneNote

Microsoft OneNote offers a robust and versatile platform for note-taking, catering to different learning and organizational styles. Here's a breakdown of the key functionalities to get you started with note-taking basics in OneNote:

Creating Notebooks and Pages:

- **Notebooks:** Organize your notes into notebooks dedicated to specific subjects, projects, or categories. Consider using a separate notebook for work, personal notes, meeting minutes, or class lectures.

- **Pages:** Within each notebook, create individual pages for specific topics or sub-categories within your broader subject. For instance, within a "Work" notebook, you might have separate pages for "Project A Meeting Notes" and "Project B Brainstorming Session."

Taking Notes:

- **Typing:** Simply click or tap anywhere on a page and start typing your notes. OneNote offers a familiar word processing experience for clear and organized text-based notes.

- **Handwriting (if applicable):** If using a touch-enabled device or a tablet with a stylus, take handwritten notes directly on the page. OneNote provides a smooth writing experience and can even convert your handwriting to text later.

- **Audio Recording:** OneNote allows you to record audio lectures, meetings, or discussions directly within your notes. This is helpful for capturing details you might miss while writing or for revisiting specific parts of a conversation later.

Adding Visuals and Information:

- **Images and Files:** Embed images, diagrams, or other files directly into your notes for visual reference and enhanced understanding. Drag and drop functionality makes it easy to incorporate these elements.

- **Drawing and Highlighting:** Use the drawing tools to sketch diagrams, highlight key points, or visually organize your notes. OneNote offers various pen colours and thicknesses for customization.

- **Web Clipping (Optional):** If using OneNote on your computer, the web clipping extension allows you to clip interesting articles or web pages directly into your notes, saving relevant online information for future reference.

Organizing Your Notes:

- **Sections (Optional):** Further organize your notes within notebooks by creating sections. For instance, within a "Class Lectures" notebook, you might have separate sections for each semester or subject.

- **Tags:** Assign relevant tags to your notes for easy searchability. This allows you to quickly find specific notes later, even if they're spread across different notebooks or pages.

- **Search Functionality:** OneNote's powerful search function lets you find specific keywords or phrases within your notes, regardless of their location.

Organizing Notebooks

Microsoft OneNote's power lies in its flexibility. But with great flexibility comes the responsibility to create a well-organized structure. Here are some strategies to keep your OneNote notebooks under control:

Categorization by Subject or Project:

- **Separate Notebooks:** Dedicate individual notebooks to broad subjects (e.g., "History Lectures," "Marketing Plan") or ongoing projects (e.g., "Client A Proposal," "Website Redesign"). This provides clear compartmentalization and simplifies navigation.

Utilizing Sections for Sub-Categories:

- **Within Notebooks:** Break down your notebooks further using sections. Sections are ideal for organizing related information within a broader subject. For instance, a "History Lectures" notebook might have sections for each semester or historical period.

Leveraging Pages for Specific Topics:

- **Within Sections:** Create individual pages for specific topics or sub-categories within your sections. This allows for granular organization and easier information retrieval. For example, within a "Marketing Plan" section, you might have separate pages for "Market Analysis," "Target Audience," and "Competitor Research."

Utilizing Tags for Cross-referencing:

- **Transcend Notebook Hierarchy:** Assign relevant tags to your notes for a flexible search system. Tags allow you to categorize information across notebooks, making it easier to find notes on a specific topic regardless of their location. For instance, you could tag notes about "Customer Segmentation" across various project notebooks.

Additional Tips:

- **Descriptive Naming:** Use clear and descriptive names for notebooks, sections, and pages to ensure you can easily identify their content at a glance.

- **Colour Coding (Optional):** Assign colours to notebooks or sections for visual differentiation and easier identification.

- **Regular Review and Archiving:** Periodically review your notebooks and archive older projects or semesters to declutter your active workspace and improve performance.

Collaboration and Sharing

Microsoft OneNote excels not just in individual note-taking, but also in fostering collaboration. Here's a breakdown of how to leverage OneNote's functionalities to work effectively with others:

Sharing Notebooks:

- **Share with Specific People:** Grant access to specific individuals by entering their email addresses. You can choose their permission level (view only, edit, or full control) to manage editing capabilities.

- **Share Links:** Generate a shareable link for your notebook, allowing anyone with the link to access it according to the permission settings you establish.

Real-Time Collaboration:

- **Simultaneous Editing:** Multiple people can work on the same page or section simultaneously. OneNote seamlessly integrates changes, ensuring everyone stays on the same page (literally).

- **Version History:** Track changes made to your notes over time. Restore previous versions if necessary.

Centralized Information Hub:

- **Project Management:** Use OneNote as a central hub for project information. Share meeting notes, brainstorm ideas, and collaborate on tasks within a single notebook.

- **Team Wikis:** Create collaborative knowledge bases or team wikis within OneNote notebooks. Capture important information, procedures, or FAQs for easy access by all team members.

Additional Tips:

- **Clear Communication:** Establish clear communication guidelines within your team regarding version control, editing etiquette, and notebook usage.

- **Comments and Mentions:** Use the commenting feature to highlight specific parts of notes and assign "@mentions" to notify specific team members.

- **Meetings and OneNote:** Integrate OneNote with online meeting platforms like Microsoft Teams. Share and collaborate on notes during meetings in real-time.

Benefits of Collaboration in OneNote:

- **Improved Efficiency:** Centralized information and real-time collaboration minimize communication overhead and streamline teamwork.

- **Enhanced Knowledge Sharing:** Team members can easily access and contribute to shared knowledge, fostering collective learning and expertise.

- **Transparency and Accountability:** Version history and clear ownership of edits ensure transparency and facilitate accountability within collaborative projects.

Integration with Other Apps

Microsoft OneNote thrives not only as a standalone application but also as a powerful integration hub, seamlessly connecting with various other apps to boost your productivity and workflow. Here's a glimpse into how OneNote integrates with other popular applications:

Microsoft Office Suite:

- **Effortless Integration:** OneNote integrates flawlessly with other Microsoft Office applications like Word, Excel, and PowerPoint. Insert content from these programs directly into your notes or vice versa, fostering a smooth workflow within the Microsoft ecosystem.

- **Linked Notes and Documents:** Create links between your OneNote notes and other Office documents for easy reference and navigation. Clicking a linked note within a Word document instantly takes you to the relevant section in OneNote.

Cloud Storage Services:

- **OneDrive Synchronization:** Store your OneNote notebooks in the cloud using OneDrive. This allows you to access your notes from any device (computer, phone, tablet) and ensures automatic syncing across all your devices.

- **Third-Party Cloud Storage:** While OneNote primarily utilizes OneDrive, some third-party cloud storage services offer unofficial integrations, allowing you to store your notebooks in alternative cloud platforms.

Task Management Apps:

- **To Do Integration:** OneNote integrates with Microsoft To Do, allowing you to create and manage tasks directly from your notes. Flag important action items within your notes and convert them into actionable tasks within To Do for seamless project management.

- **Third-Party Task Apps:** Several third-party task management applications offer integrations with OneNote through add-ins or Zapier automation. This allows you to connect your preferred task management system with OneNote for a more unified workflow.

Additional Integration Options:

- **Web Clipper Extensions:** OneNote web clipper extensions for various browsers allow you to clip interesting articles, web pages, or specific sections of websites directly into your notes, saving relevant online information for future reference.

- **Email Integration (limited):** While not a direct feature, some third-party add-ins or browser extensions allow you to clip emails or specific portions of emails and send them to OneNote for note-taking purposes.

Benefits of App Integration:

- **Streamlined Workflow:** Integrating OneNote with other apps you already use minimizes the need to switch between applications and promotes a more efficient workflow.

- **Centralized Information Management:** Consolidate information from various sources within your OneNote notebooks, creating a central hub for all your project-related content.

- **Enhanced Functionality:** Leverage the strengths of different applications to create a more powerful and versatile note-taking and information management system.

Exploring Integration Options:

The specific integration options available depend on the applications you use. Research the app stores for your devices or the official websites of the applications you wish to connect with OneNote to discover available integrations and functionalities.

By understanding how OneNote integrates with other apps, you can unlock its full potential and create a customized workflow that caters to your specific needs and preferences. Remember, effective integration is about creating a system that works for you, so explore the possibilities and unleash the power of OneNote!

CHAPTER FOUR
Additional Application

4.1 Microsoft Teams

Microsoft Teams is a powerful collaboration application developed by Microsoft, designed to streamline communication and teamwork within organizations. It functions as a central hub, integrating various functionalities like chat, video conferencing, file sharing, task management, and app integration, all under one roof. Here's a breakdown of the key features and benefits of Microsoft Teams:

Communication Channels:

- **Team Chats:** Foster ongoing communication within specific teams or departments through dedicated chat channels. Share messages, ideas, and files for real-time collaboration.

- **Video Conferencing:** Conduct high-quality video meetings with individuals or groups. Screen sharing, breakout rooms, and live captions enhance the meeting experience.

- **Audio Calling:** Make and receive voice calls directly within Teams, eliminating the need for traditional phone calls and promoting seamless communication.

Collaboration Features:

- **File Sharing:** Share documents, spreadsheets, presentations, and other files within Teams channels or chats. Collaborate on files in real-time with co-editing functionality.

- **Task Management:** Assign tasks to team members, track progress, and set deadlines directly within Teams. Improve project visibility and accountability.

- **Meetings and Agendas:** Schedule meetings, create agendas, and share notes within Teams, keeping everyone informed and aligned.

Additional functionalities:

- **Integrations:** Expand functionality by integrating Teams with various third-party apps like Trello, Salesforce, and Dropbox, centralizing your workflow within Teams.

- **Cloud Storage:** Leverage OneDrive cloud storage to access, share, and collaborate on files from any device.

- **Security and Compliance:** Microsoft Teams adheres to strict security protocols to safeguard sensitive information and comply with industry regulations.

Benefits of Using Microsoft Teams:

- **Enhanced Communication:** Centralized channels, chat functionalities, and video conferencing promote clear and efficient communication within teams.

- **Improved Collaboration:** Real-time co-editing of documents, task management tools, and shared files streamline collaboration and project execution.

- **Increased Productivity:** Seamless integration of communication, collaboration, and task management tools within a single platform minimizes context switching and boosts productivity.

- **Accessibility and Flexibility:** Access Teams from your desktop, phone, or web browser, enabling collaboration and communication from anywhere, anytime.

Is Microsoft Teams Right for You?

Microsoft Teams is a valuable tool for organizations of all sizes, particularly those that rely on teamwork and real-time communication. If your organization or team struggles with communication silos, inefficient collaboration processes, or scattered project management tools, then Microsoft Teams can be a game-changer.

Getting Started with Microsoft Teams:

If your organization uses Microsoft 365, you likely already have access to Microsoft Teams. Download the application or access it through the web browser. Explore the interface, familiarize yourself with the functionalities, and start collaborating with your team!

By leveraging the strengths of Microsoft Teams, you can foster a more connected, collaborative, and productive work environment for your team or organization.

4.2 Microsoft OneDrive

Microsoft OneDrive is a cloud storage service developed by Microsoft. It allows you to store your files (documents, photos, videos, etc.) online and access them from any device with an internet connection. OneDrive integrates seamlessly with other Microsoft applications and services, making it a popular choice for individuals and businesses alike. Here's a closer look at OneDrive's key features and benefits:

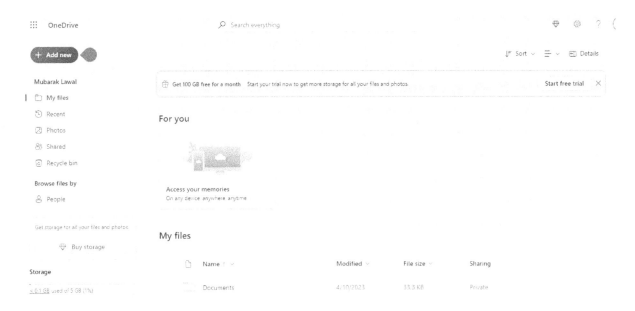

File Storage and Access:

- **Upload and Store Files:** Upload various file types (documents, photos, videos) to your OneDrive storage space. Access these files from any device (computer, phone, tablet) with the OneDrive app or web interface.

- **Cloud Backup:** OneDrive safeguards your files from device failures or accidental deletion by storing them securely in the cloud.

Sharing and Collaboration:

- **Share Files and Folders:** Easily share files and folders with others by inviting them through email. Set permission levels (view only, edit) to control access.

- **Real-time Collaboration:** Collaborate on documents in real-time with others. Microsoft Office applications within OneDrive allow multiple users to edit files simultaneously.

Integration with Microsoft Services:

- **Seamless Integration:** OneDrive integrates smoothly with other Microsoft services like Word, Excel, PowerPoint, and Outlook. Save your documents directly to OneDrive from within these applications for effortless cloud storage and access.

- **Centralized Hub:** Use OneDrive as a central hub for storing and managing all your work-related files, accessible from any device you use with Microsoft applications.

Additional Features:

- **Automatic File Syncing:** Enable automatic file syncing to ensure your files are always up-to-date across all your devices. Any changes you make to a file on one device are automatically reflected in the cloud and on your other devices.

- **Offline File Access:** With OneDrive, you can access certain files even when you're offline. Mark important files for offline access, allowing you to work on them even without an internet connection.

- **Security and Version Control:** OneDrive employs robust security measures to protect your files. Version history allows you to revert to previous versions of files if needed.

Free and Paid Storage Plans:

- **Free Storage:** Microsoft offers a free OneDrive plan with a limited storage quota (typically 5GB). This can be sufficient for basic needs.

- **Paid Storage Plans:** For additional storage space, you can upgrade to a paid OneDrive plan with more storage capacity, catering to users with extensive file collections.

Benefits of Using Microsoft OneDrive:

- **Accessibility:** Access your files from anywhere, anytime, with any internet-connected device.

- **Backup and Security:** Safeguard your files from device failures or loss with secure cloud storage.

- **Collaboration:** Collaborate on documents with ease and in real-time with colleagues or classmates.

- **Integration:** Seamless integration with Microsoft services streamlines your workflow and centralizes file management.

Who is OneDrive For?

OneDrive is a versatile cloud storage solution suitable for various users:

- **Individuals:** Store personal documents, photos, and videos for safekeeping and access from any device.

- **Businesses:** Facilitate secure file storage, collaboration, and document management for teams.

- **Students:** Collaborate on projects and assignments with classmates, store notes and coursework securely.

Getting Started with OneDrive:

If you have a Microsoft account (Outlook, Hotmail, etc.), you already have access to OneDrive with free storage space. Sign in to your account online or download the OneDrive app to your devices. Start uploading your files and experience the convenience and security of cloud storage!

In conclusion, Microsoft OneDrive offers a reliable and user-friendly cloud storage solution, integrated seamlessly with the broader Microsoft ecosystem. Its features cater to both individual and business needs, making it a valuable tool for storing, accessing, and collaborating on your important files.

4.3 Microsoft SharePoint

Microsoft SharePoint is a web-based platform designed to empower organizations to manage content, knowledge, and applications. It goes beyond simple file storage like OneDrive and offers a comprehensive suite of functionalities to facilitate collaboration, communication, and streamline internal processes. Here's a breakdown of SharePoint's key features and how it benefits businesses:

Content Management:

- **Document Libraries:** Create central repositories for storing, organizing, and sharing various documents (reports, presentations, proposals) within teams or departments.

- **Version Control:** Track changes made to documents over time and revert to previous versions if necessary, ensuring information accuracy.

- **Metadata and Search:** Assign metadata (tags, categories) to documents for better organization and information retrieval. Leverage powerful search functionalities to find specific content efficiently.

Collaboration and Communication:

- **Team Sites:** Establish dedicated websites for teams or projects. Share documents, news updates, announcements, and calendars within a centralized hub, fostering collaboration and information sharing.

- **Workflows and Automation:** Set up automated workflows to streamline repetitive tasks (e.g., document approval processes). This frees up time for employees to focus on more strategic work.

- **Integration with Teams:** SharePoint integrates with Microsoft Teams, allowing you to access and collaborate on documents directly within Teams channels, fostering seamless communication and teamwork.

Customization and Flexibility:

- **Customizable Sites:** Create custom layouts and functionalities for team sites using web parts (pre-built building blocks) to cater to specific team needs and workflows.

- **Third-Party Add-ins:** Extend SharePoint's functionalities with a vast library of third-party add-ins, creating a solution tailored to your specific business requirements.

Security and Administration:

- **Role-Based Access Control:** Set granular permissions for users and groups, controlling access to specific sites, document libraries, or files based on their roles within the organization.

- **Compliance Features:** SharePoint offers features to support data security and compliance with various industry regulations.

Benefits of Using Microsoft SharePoint:

- **Improved Collaboration:** Centralized document storage, communication tools, and team sites foster collaboration and knowledge sharing within teams.

- **Enhanced Productivity:** Automated workflows, powerful search, and role-based access control streamline tasks and processes, boosting overall productivity.

- **Reduced Costs:** SharePoint can potentially reduce reliance on physical document storage and improve information accessibility, leading to cost savings.

- **Scalability and Security:** SharePoint scales to accommodate the needs of growing organizations while maintaining robust security measures to protect sensitive information.

Is Microsoft SharePoint Right for Your Business?

SharePoint is a versatile platform that caters to businesses of all sizes. It's particularly valuable for organizations that:

- Struggle with document sprawl and information silos across departments.

- Seek to improve collaboration and communication within teams.

- Require streamlined document management and automated workflows.

- Have a growing need for a secure and scalable content management system.

Getting Started with Microsoft SharePoint:

SharePoint is typically included in Microsoft 365 Business and Enterprise plans. If your organization has an active Microsoft 365 subscription, you likely already have access to SharePoint. Your IT administrator can set up your SharePoint environment and provide training for your users.

By leveraging the strengths of Microsoft SharePoint, organizations can create a centralized hub for collaboration, streamline information management, and empower employees to work more efficiently and effectively.

4.4 Microsoft Access

Microsoft Access is a database management system (DBMS) from Microsoft. It empowers users to create and manage databases, which are essentially electronic filing systems that store, organize, and retrieve information in a structured format. Unlike spreadsheets like Excel, Access is specifically designed for relational databases, allowing you to establish connections between different data sets for more complex queries and analysis.

Key functionalities of Microsoft Access:

- **Database Creation:** Design and build databases using tables, forms, queries, and reports. Tables store your data in a structured format with rows and columns.

- **Data Manipulation:** Add, edit, delete, and manage data within your database tables.

- **Relationships and Queries:** Create relationships between tables based on shared fields. Utilize queries to retrieve specific data or perform calculations based on your criteria.

- **Forms and Reports:** Design user-friendly forms for data entry and modification. Create reports to summarize and present your data in a visually appealing format.

- **Customization:** Customize the appearance and functionalities of your database using Access' built-in tools.

Benefits of Using Microsoft Access:

- **Efficient Data Management:** Organize large amounts of data effectively, minimizing redundancy and ensuring data accuracy.

- **Powerful Queries and Analysis:** Extract specific data sets, perform calculations, and gain insights from your data through powerful queries and reports.

- **Improved Decision-Making:** Data analysis capabilities within Access can inform better decision-making processes within your organization.

- **Customization and Automation:** Customize your database to match your specific needs and automate repetitive tasks for increased efficiency.

Who Can Benefit from Microsoft Access?

- **Small Businesses:** Manage customer information, inventory, or project data efficiently.

- **Non-profit Organizations:** Track donors, volunteers, or program activity data.

- **Schools and Universities:** Maintain student records, course information, or library catalogs.

- **Individuals:** Organize personal collections, finances, or project information.

Limitations of Microsoft Access:

- **Complexity for Beginners:** Access can have a steeper learning curve compared to simpler spreadsheet applications.

- **Scalability Limitations:** While suitable for small and medium-sized databases, Access might not be ideal for extremely large or complex data sets requiring enterprise-level solutions.

Is Microsoft Access Right for You?

Consider these factors to determine if Access meets your needs:

- **Data Volume and Complexity:** If you manage a large amount of interrelated data and require complex queries or analysis, Access can be a valuable tool.

- **Existing Software:** If you already use Microsoft products extensively, Access integrates well within the Microsoft ecosystem.

- **Technical Expertise:** Be prepared to invest time in learning the fundamentals of database design and Access functionalities.

Learning Resources:

Microsoft provides various resources and tutorials to help you get started with Access. There are also numerous online courses and communities dedicated to Access training.

Microsoft Access offers a powerful and versatile solution for data management. While it has a learning curve, its ability to organize, analyse, and generate reports from your data can significantly enhance your productivity and decision-making capabilities. If you're looking to move beyond spreadsheets and delve into the world of relational databases, Microsoft Access is a valuable tool to consider.

4.5 Microsoft Publisher

Microsoft Publisher is a software program designed for creating professional-looking publications like brochures, flyers, newsletters, postcards, and greetings cards. It offers a user-friendly interface that caters to those without extensive graphic design experience.

Key functionalities of Microsoft Publisher:

- **Templates and Layouts:** Get started quickly with a wide variety of pre-designed templates for different publication types.

- **Drag-and-Drop Design:** Easily add and arrange text, images, shapes, and clip art using a drag-and-drop interface. No coding knowledge required.

- **Design Tools:** Utilize built-in design tools to format text, adjust layouts, and apply effects for a polished look.

- **Mail Merge:** Personalize mass mailings by integrating with Microsoft Word for mail merge functionality.

- **Image Editing:** Perform basic image editing tasks like cropping, resizing, and adjusting brightness/contrast directly within Publisher.

Who can benefit from Microsoft Publisher?

- **Small Businesses and Organizations:** Create professional marketing materials, newsletters, or event flyers without needing expensive design software.

- **Educators and Students:** Design engaging presentations, classroom handouts, or school newsletters.

- **Individuals:** Craft personalized greeting cards, invitations, or flyers for personal events.

Limitations of Microsoft Publisher:

- **Limited Design Flexibility:** While offering user-friendliness, Publisher might not provide the same level of design customization as professional graphic design applications like Adobe InDesign.

- **Focus on Print Design:** Publisher primarily focuses on creating print publications. It may not be ideal for complex digital content creation.

- **Planned Discontinuation:** Microsoft announced plans to discontinue support for Publisher in October 2026.

Alternatives to Microsoft Publisher:

- **Adobe InDesign:** Industry-standard graphic design software offering extensive design flexibility but with a steeper learning curve.

- **Canva:** Free online design platform with user-friendly templates and tools for creating various visuals. Limited offline functionality.

- **Google Slides:** Free presentation software with basic design functionalities suitable for simple publications or presentations.

Is Microsoft Publisher Right for You?

Consider these factors when deciding if Microsoft Publisher is a suitable choice:

- **Design Needs:** If you require basic design capabilities for print publications and prioritize ease of use, Publisher can be a good option.

- **Budget:** Publisher is included in some Microsoft 365 subscriptions or available as a one-time purchase. Consider free alternatives if budget is a concern.

- **Technical Expertise:** Publisher offers a user-friendly interface suitable for beginners in design.

Microsoft Publisher remains a valuable tool for those seeking to create professional-looking publications without needing extensive design expertise. However, with its planned discontinuation in October 2026, you might want to consider alternative solutions depending on your future needs and the longevity of your chosen software.

CHAPTER FIVE
Advanced Features

5.1 Office 365 Admin Centre

The Microsoft 365 Admin Centre (sometimes referred to as the admin portal) is a web-based management console that empowers IT administrators to oversee their organization's Microsoft 365 environment. It functions as a central hub for managing users, licenses, security settings, services, and various other aspects that contribute to a smooth and secure cloud experience.

Key Functionalities of the Admin Centre:

- **User and License Management:**

  o   Create, edit, and deactivate user accounts.

  o   Assign appropriate Microsoft 365 licenses with specific functionalities to each user based on their needs.

  o   Manage user groups for simplified permission assignment and streamlined license allocation.

  o   Grant or restrict access to specific services (like Exchange Online, SharePoint Online, Teams, etc.) for individual users or groups.

- **Security and Compliance:**

  o   Implement robust security measures like multi-factor authentication (MFA) to fortify login security.

  o   Configure data encryption at rest and in transit to safeguard sensitive information.

  o   Set up data loss prevention policies to minimize the risk of accidental or unauthorized data leaks.

  o   Manage eDiscovery and auditing tools to search for and export electronic data for legal or compliance purposes.

  o   Control access to sensitive data by implementing data classification and access restrictions.

- **Deployment and Management:**

  o   Manage the installation and configuration of Office applications on user devices.

  o   Oversee mobile device management (MDM) policies and configurations for devices accessing your organization's Microsoft 365 data.

  o   Control data sharing by setting external sharing permissions to govern how users can share data with people outside your organization.

- **Monitoring and Analytics:**

  o Monitor the health status of various Microsoft 365 services to identify and address potential issues promptly.

  o Gain insights into user activity reports for different Microsoft 365 services, allowing you to track trends and optimize user behaviour.

  o Analyse license usage patterns to optimize your subscription costs and ensure efficient resource allocation.

- **Additional Features:**

  o Submit support tickets to Microsoft for troubleshooting assistance.

  o Manage your Microsoft 365 subscription plan, view billing information, and make changes if necessary.

  o Access helpful documentation, training materials, and support resources from Microsoft.

Accessing the Admin Centre:

The Microsoft 365 Admin Centre can be accessed through a web browser at. you'll need a user account with administrative privileges for your organization's Microsoft 365 subscription.

Benefits of Utilizing the Admin Centre:

- **Centralized Management:** Simplifies the administration of all Microsoft 365 services from a single, unified platform.

- **Enhanced Security:** Provides tools to implement robust security measures and ensure user and data protection.

- **Improved Compliance:** Offers features to facilitate adherence to organizational data governance and legal regulations.

- **Streamlined User Management:** Enables efficient user provisioning, license assignment, and permission control.

- **Cost Optimization:** Allows you to monitor license usage and optimize your subscription plan to avoid unnecessary costs.

- **Data-driven Decision Making:** Provides access to user activity reports and insights that can inform strategic decisions.

By leveraging the Microsoft 365 Admin Centre effectively, IT administrators can empower their users, safeguard sensitive data, optimize resources, and ensure a productive and secure cloud environment for their organization.

5.2 Integrations and Add-ins

In Microsoft 365, integrations and add-ins extend the functionalities of the familiar Office applications (Word, Excel, PowerPoint, Outlook, etc.) They allow you to connect to external services, automate workflows, and access specialized tools directly within your Office environment.

Here's a breakdown of the two categories:

Microsoft 365 Integrations:

- **Built-in Integrations:** Microsoft 365 offers built-in integrations with various Microsoft services like OneDrive, SharePoint, and Teams. These integrations allow you to seamlessly access and collaborate on files stored in these cloud services directly from within Office applications.

- **Third-party Integrations:** Microsoft provides an open platform for developers to create custom integrations for Microsoft 365. These integrations connect you to a vast array of external services, such as cloud storage providers (Dropbox, Box), project management tools (Asana, Trello), CRM systems (Salesforce, Zendesk), and many more.

Benefits of Microsoft 365 Integrations:

- **Streamlined Workflows:** Automate repetitive tasks and connect different applications to create seamless workflows.

- **Increased Efficiency:** Enhance productivity by eliminating the need to switch between different applications for tasks.

- **Centralized Data Management:** Manage and access all your data from within a familiar Office environment.

- **Improved Collaboration:** Facilitate collaboration with colleagues and external partners by leveraging integrated tools.

Finding and Using Integrations:

- **Microsoft AppSource:** The Microsoft AppSource store is the official marketplace for third-party add-ins and integrations compatible with Microsoft 365 applications. You can search for integrations by category, functionality, or application.

- **Within Office Applications:** Some Office applications (like Outlook) have a built-in "Get Add-ins" or "Store" section where you can browse and install popular integrations directly.

Microsoft 365 Add-ins:

- **Definition:** Add-ins are small applications that extend the functionalities of specific Office applications. They can add new features, automate tasks, or provide specialized tools tailored to your needs.

- **Examples:**

  - ○ Grammarly add-in for enhanced grammar and spell checking within Word documents.

  - ○ DocuSign add-in for electronic signatures within documents.

  - ○ Salesforce Lightning add-in for managing Salesforce data directly from Excel.

Benefits of Microsoft 365 Add-ins:

- **Customization:** Tailor your Office experience by adding functionalities specific to your workflow or industry.

- **Task Automation:** Automate repetitive tasks to save time and effort.

- **Specialized Tools:** Gain access to specialized features that may not be natively available within Office applications.

Finding and Using Add-ins:

- **Similar to integrations, you can find add-ins through the Microsoft AppSource store or directly within the "Get Add-ins" section of your Office applications.**

Security Considerations:

- **Review Permissions:** Always review the permissions requested by an add-in before installing it. Grant only the necessary permissions to ensure data security.

- **Reputable Developers:** Choose add-ins from reputable developers with positive user reviews to minimize security risks.

By effectively leveraging integrations and add-ins, you can transform your Microsoft 365 experience into a powerful and versatile productivity hub that caters to your specific needs and workflows. Explore the vast options available and customize your Office environment to streamline your work, boost collaboration, and achieve greater efficiency.

5.3 Mobile Applications

Microsoft 365 offers a suite of mobile applications that allow you to access your documents, emails, calendars, and other functionalities on the go from your smartphone or tablet. These applications are available for both Android and iOS devices. Here's a rundown of the key mobile applications included in most Microsoft 365 subscriptions:

- **Microsoft Word:** Create, view, and edit Word documents on your mobile device.

- **Microsoft Excel:** Create, view, and edit Excel spreadsheets on your mobile device.

- **Microsoft PowerPoint:** Create, view, and edit PowerPoint presentations on your mobile device.

- **Microsoft OneNote:** Capture notes, ideas, and to-do lists with OneNote, accessible from any device.

- **Microsoft Outlook:** Manage your email, calendar, and contacts directly from your phone or tablet.

- **Microsoft OneDrive:** Store, access, and share your files from anywhere with cloud storage.

- **Microsoft Teams:** Collaborate with colleagues, hold meetings, chat, and share files using Teams on your mobile device.

Benefits of Using Mobile Apps:

- **Productivity on the Go:** Work on documents, emails, or projects from anywhere with an internet connection.

- **Real-time Collaboration:** Collaborate on documents and projects with colleagues in real-time, even when you're not in the same location.

- **Offline Access:** Certain features within some apps (like viewing documents or working on local drafts) may function even without an internet connection.

- **Mobile-Specific Features:** The mobile apps offer some functionalities optimized for touchscreens and smaller device formats.

Getting Started with Mobile Apps:

1. Download the Microsoft Office mobile app or individual application from the App Store (iOS) or Google Play Store (Android).

2. Sign in with your Microsoft 365 username and password.

3. The specific functionalities available within the mobile apps may vary depending on your Microsoft 365 subscription plan.

Additional Points to Consider:

- **Internet Connection:** For optimal functionality, an internet connection is recommended.

- **File Storage:** Be mindful of your OneDrive storage quota when using the mobile apps.

- **Security:** Ensure you have a strong password or PIN set up for your mobile device to protect your data.

Overall, the Microsoft 365 mobile applications offer a powerful and convenient way to stay productive and connected while you're away from your desk. They allow you to access your work documents, collaborate with colleagues, and manage your schedule, all from your smartphone or tablet.

CHAPTER SIX
Troubleshooting and Support

6.1 Common Issues and Solutions

Here's a breakdown of some common issues you might encounter while using Office 365 and troubleshooting solutions you can try:

Installation and Activation Issues:

- **Problem:** Installation fails or takes too long.

- **Solution:** Check your internet connection and ensure you meet the minimum system requirements. Try restarting your device and running the installation as an administrator. You can also download the offline installer directly from Microsoft.

- **Problem:** Activation errors occur.

- **Solution:** Verify you're using the correct login credentials and that your Microsoft 365 subscription is active. Ensure your device's date and time settings are accurate. If you have recently migrated from a different version of Office, you may need to uninstall the old version before activating the new one.

Sign-in Problems:

- **Problem:** Unable to sign in to Office 365 applications.

- **Solution:** Double-check your username and password. Consider resetting your password if needed. Check if two-factor authentication (MFA) is enabled for your account and complete the additional verification step. Ensure you have a stable internet connection.

Synchronization Issues (OneDrive & OneDrive for Business):

- **Problem:** Files are not syncing correctly between your device and OneDrive.

- **Solution:** Check your internet connection. Restart the OneDrive desktop application. Pause and then resume syncing. In some cases, you may need to unlink and then relink your OneDrive account.

Access and Permission Issues:

- **Problem:** You cannot access or edit a file or folder stored in SharePoint or OneDrive.

- **Solution:** Verify that you have the necessary permissions granted by the owner of the file or folder. Contact the owner to request access if needed.

Error Messages:

- **Problem:** You encounter various error messages within Office 365 applications.

- **Solution:** The specific solution depends on the error message itself. However, some general troubleshooting steps include restarting the application, repairing the Office installation, or checking for and installing the latest updates. You can also search online for the specific error code to find more targeted solutions from Microsoft support resources.

Additional Tips:

- **Update Regularly:** Keep Microsoft 365 applications and your operating system updated with the latest security patches and bug fixes.

- **Restart Your Device:** A simple restart can often resolve temporary glitches.

- **Microsoft Support:** If you've exhausted all troubleshooting options, you can reach out to Microsoft support for further assistance. They offer various resources like online documentation, support forums, and chat support with technicians.

By following these tips and solutions, you can address many common issues that arise while using Office 365. Remember, the specific troubleshooting steps may vary depending on the exact nature of the problem you're encountering.

6.2 Accessing Office 365 Support

Self-Help Resources

1. **Microsoft Support Website:**

   - Visit support.microsoft.com to access a wide range of articles, tutorials, and troubleshooting guides for Office 365.

2. **Office 365 Help Centre:**

   - Go to support.office.com for specific support on Office 365 applications. This site includes FAQs, how-to videos, and community forums.

3. **In-App Help:**

   - Use the help features built into Office 365 applications. Click the Help icon (usually a question mark or "?" symbol) in the ribbon to search for answers or access guided tutorials.

Online Community and Forums

1. Microsoft Community:

   - Visit the Microsoft Community to ask questions and find answers from other users and Microsoft experts.

2. TechNet and MSDN Forums:

- For more technical inquiries, visit the TechNet and MSDN forums to engage with IT professionals and developers.

Contacting Support

1. Office 365 Admin Centre:

   - If you are an Office 365 admin, log in to the Office 365 Admin Centre to access support options. From the dashboard, navigate to Support > New service request to create a support ticket.

2. Phone Support:

   - Contact Microsoft Support by phone. You can find the relevant phone numbers by visiting the Microsoft Support Contact page.

3. Live Chat:

   - Use the live chat option available on the Microsoft Support website for real-time assistance with a support agent.

Additional Support Options

1. Microsoft Virtual Agent:

   - Utilize the Microsoft Virtual Agent, an AI-driven chatbot available on the Microsoft Support website, to get immediate answers to common issues and questions.

2. Training and Webinars:

   - Access free training sessions and webinars offered by Microsoft to learn more about Office 365 features and best practices. Visit the Microsoft Training page for more information.

3. Partner Support:

   - If you purchased Office 365 through a Microsoft partner, you might be able to access additional support and resources directly from the partner.

By using these resources, you can efficiently find help and support for any issues or questions you may have regarding Office 365.

6.3 Community Resources and Forums

Microsoft offers a variety of community resources and forums where you can connect with other users, get help with problems, and learn new tips and tricks for using Microsoft 365. Here are some of the most valuable ones:

Official Microsoft Forums:

- **Microsoft 365 community:** This is the official Microsoft forum dedicated to Microsoft 365 discussions. Here you can find threads on a wide range of topics, from general usage questions to specific application troubleshooting.

- **Microsoft Tech Community:** A broader forum that encompasses all Microsoft products and services, including discussions related to Office 365 applications.

Benefits of Official Forums:

- **Direct Connection with Microsoft:** Product experts and support engineers from Microsoft sometimes participate in these forums, offering official guidance and solutions.

- **Large Community:** With a vast user base, you're more likely to find someone who has faced a similar issue and can share their solution.

- **Wide Range of Topics:** Discussions cover almost every aspect of Microsoft 365, from beginner questions to advanced functionalities.

Alternative Community Resources:

- **Reddit Communities:** Subreddits like r/Office365 and r/Microsoft365 offer active communities where users can ask questions, share experiences, and get help from other users.

- **Social Media Groups:** Look for Facebook groups or LinkedIn groups dedicated to Microsoft 365 discussions. These groups can provide a more informal setting for questions and knowledge sharing.

- **Tech Blogs and Websites:** Many technology blogs and websites focus on Microsoft 365 and offer tutorials, troubleshooting guides, and discussions in the comment sections.

Tips for Using Community Resources:

- **Search Before Posting:** Before creating a new thread, search the forums to see if your question has already been answered. This saves time and avoids duplicate posts.

- **Provide Details:** When asking a question, be specific about the problem you're facing. Include details like the application you're using, the error message you encountered (if any), and what troubleshooting steps you've already tried. The more information you provide, the easier it will be for others to assist you.

- **Be Polite and Respectful:** Maintain a professional and courteous tone in your interactions within the forums.

- **Share Your Knowledge:** Once you've found a solution or gained valuable insights, consider helping others by answering questions or sharing your experience.

By leveraging these community resources and forums, you can tap into a wealth of knowledge and support from a vast network of Microsoft 365 users and experts.

6.4 Keeping Office 365 Updated

Here's how to keep Microsoft 365 (Office 365) updated to ensure you have the latest features, security patches, and bug fixes:

Automatic Updates (Recommended):

By default, Microsoft 365 is configured for automatic updates. This is the most convenient and secure way to stay up-to-date. There are two main update channels for automatic updates:

- **Current Channel:** Receives the latest updates monthly, providing access to new features and functionalities as soon as they become available.

- **Deferred Channel (Optional):** Provides a more conservative update approach, receiving security patches and bug fixes a few months after the Current Channel. This allows for additional testing and reduces the risk of encountering unforeseen issues with new features.

Checking for Updates Manually:

Even with automatic updates enabled, you can manually check for updates at any time:

1. Open any Office application (Word, Excel, PowerPoint, etc.).
2. Click on **File** or **Account** (depending on the application).
3. Go to **Account** or **Office Account**.
4. Under **Product Information**, click on **Update Options**.
5. Select **Update Now**.

Admin Control for Business Users:

If you're an administrator for a Microsoft 365 business subscription, you can manage update settings for users within your organization from the Microsoft 365 admin centre. This allows you to choose the update channel (Current or Deferred) and configure update policies for different user groups.

Benefits of Keeping Office 365 Updated:

- **Improved Security:** Updates often include critical security patches that address vulnerabilities and protect your data from cyber threats.

- **New Features and Functionality:** Automatic updates ensure you have access to the latest features and functionalities as they are rolled out by Microsoft.

- **Bug Fixes and Performance Improvements:** Updates often address bugs and performance issues, improving the overall stability and responsiveness of Office applications.

Here are some additional points to consider:

- **Update Notifications:** Microsoft may display notifications within the applications when new updates are available.

- **Restart Required:** In some cases, updates may require you to restart your computer to complete the installation process.

- **Internet Connection:** An active internet connection is necessary to download and install updates.

By enabling automatic updates or checking for updates manually at regular intervals, you can ensure your Office 365 installation is always up-to-date and secure.

CHAPTER SEVEN
Best Practices

7.1 Optimizing Productivity with Office 365

Here are some ways you can optimize your productivity using Microsoft 365 (formerly Office 365):

Leveraging Collaboration Features:

- **Real-time co-authoring:** Work on documents, spreadsheets, and presentations simultaneously with colleagues, eliminating the need for multiple versions and back-and-forth emailing. Utilize features like comments and suggestions for seamless collaboration within Microsoft Word, Excel, and PowerPoint.

- **Microsoft Teams:** Use Teams as your central hub for communication and project management. Create channels for specific projects or departments, hold video meetings, share files, and collaborate on tasks in real-time.

- **OneDrive and SharePoint:** Store and share files centrally with colleagues. OneDrive provides individual cloud storage, while SharePoint offers team-based document libraries with access controls. This eliminates confusion about where to find the latest version of a document.

Optimizing Workflows and Automation:

- **Power Automate:** Automate repetitive tasks using Power Automate (formerly Flow). This can include things like sending notifications, collecting data, or copying files. Free up valuable time by automating manual processes.

- **Templates:** Utilize pre-built templates for documents, presentations, and spreadsheets in Microsoft Office applications. These templates can save you time and ensure a consistent format for your work.

- **Outlook Features:** Take advantage of features like Focused Inbox and email scheduling in Outlook to prioritize important messages and manage your email flow more efficiently.

Effective Time Management and Organization:

- **Microsoft To Do:** Consolidate your tasks and to-do lists using Microsoft To Do. Create lists for different projects or areas of responsibility, set due dates, and track progress.

- **Planner in Teams:** Use the Planner tab within Teams to create task boards, assign tasks to team members, track progress, and collaborate on projects visually.

- **Calendar Integration:** Schedule appointments, meetings, and deadlines across your Outlook calendar and integrate it with your Teams schedule for a holistic view of your commitments.

Enhancing Communication and Knowledge Sharing:

- **Microsoft Stream:** Utilize Stream, a secure video platform within Microsoft 365, to record and share presentations, training videos, or internal announcements with colleagues.

- **Yammer:** Foster knowledge sharing and discussions within your organization using Yammer, an enterprise social network platform.

Utilizing AI Features:

- **Intelligent Search:** Leverage the improved search functionalities in Microsoft 365 applications to quickly find the information you need across your emails, documents, and OneDrive storage.

- **Ideas Feature in PowerPoint:** Use the Ideas feature in PowerPoint to suggest design improvements, data insights, and writing style suggestions for your presentations.

Additional Tips:

- **Customize your workspace:** Personalize your Microsoft 365 experience by taking advantage of keyboard shortcuts, customizing your workspace layout, and utilizing features like text-to-speech or Immersive Reader for improved accessibility.

- **Explore third-party add-ins:** The Microsoft 365 app store offers a variety of third-party add-ins that can extend the functionalities of the applications and cater to your specific needs.

- **Stay updated:** Take advantage of online training resources and webinars offered by Microsoft to learn new features and optimize your use of Microsoft 365 applications.

By implementing these strategies, you can leverage the full potential of Microsoft 365 to streamline workflows, collaborate effectively, manage your time efficiently, and ultimately achieve greater productivity in your work.

7.2 Security and Privacy Tips

Microsoft 365 offers a robust suite of tools, but it's important to be mindful of security and privacy to protect your data and organization. Here are some key tips:

Multi-Factor Authentication (MFA):

- This is the single most important step. Enable MFA for all user accounts in your organization. MFA adds an extra layer of security beyond just a username and password, making it much harder for unauthorized access.

- There are various MFA methods, like verification codes sent via text message or mobile app notifications.

Strong Passwords and Password Management:

- Enforce strong password policies within your organization. This includes minimum password length, complexity requirements, and regular password changes.

- Avoid using the same password for different accounts and avoid easily guessable personal information.

- Consider using a password manager to securely store and manage complex passwords.

Data Encryption:

- Microsoft 365 offers data encryption at rest and in transit. However, you may want to consider additional encryption layers for highly sensitive data.

Admin Controls and User Permissions:

- Utilize the Microsoft 365 admin centre to manage user accounts, assign permissions, and restrict access to sensitive data and functionalities based on the principle of least privilege (users only have access to what they need for their job).

- Regularly review and update user permissions to ensure they remain appropriate.

Beware of Phishing Attacks:

- Phishing emails are a common tactic used by cybercriminals to steal login credentials. Be cautious of emails requesting personal information or urging you to click on suspicious links.

- Educate users within your organization about phishing attempts and best practices for identifying them.

Monitor User Activity and Alerts:

- Configure alert notifications for suspicious activities like failed login attempts or unauthorized access attempts. This allows for early detection and mitigation of potential security breaches.

Data Backup and Recovery:

- Regularly back up your data to an external source in case of accidental deletion, ransomware attacks, or other unforeseen circumstances.

- Microsoft 365 offers some data recovery options, but having an independent backup is crucial.

Staying Informed:

- Keep Microsoft 365 applications and your operating system updated with the latest security patches to address vulnerabilities.

- Stay informed about emerging security threats and best practices by following reputable security blogs or attending webinars.

Privacy Considerations:

- Be mindful of the data you store in Microsoft 365 cloud services.

- Understand Microsoft's data privacy policies and how your data is used.

- If you handle sensitive data, explore additional privacy-enhancing features or tools offered by Microsoft or third-party providers.

By following these security and privacy best practices, you can leverage the power of Microsoft 365 with confidence, protecting your organization's data and user privacy in the cloud environment.

7.3 Backup and Data Recovery

While Microsoft 365 offers built-in redundancy and some data recovery options, it's crucial to have a comprehensive backup and data recovery strategy in place for several reasons:

- **Accidental Deletion:** Users can accidentally delete files or emails in Microsoft 365. The built-in recovery options typically only extend to a limited timeframe.

- **Security Threats:** Ransomware attacks or other security incidents can encrypt or corrupt your data. Having backups allows you to restore data from a clean, uninfected point.

- **Compliance Needs:** Depending on your industry or regulations, you may need to retain data for a specific period. Backups ensure you have access to this data even if it's deleted from the primary storage location.

Here's a breakdown of backup and data recovery considerations for Microsoft 365:

Microsoft's Built-in Features:

- **Version History:** Microsoft 365 offers version history for most file types, allowing you to restore previous versions of documents, spreadsheets, or presentations for a limited time (typically 30 days).

- **Recycle Bin:** Deleted emails and OneDrive files go to a recycle bin for a period before permanent deletion. The recycle bin retention period can be configured by an administrator.

Limitations of Built-in Options:

- Recovery periods for version history and recycle bin are finite. Data deleted beyond that timeframe may be unrecoverable.

- These features don't protect against security threats like ransomware attacks that encrypt your data.

Implementing a Backup Solution:

- **Third-party Backup Services:** Several third-party vendors offer backup solutions specifically designed for Microsoft 365. These solutions can back up your data to a separate cloud storage location, providing an additional layer of protection.

- **Backup to On-Premises Storage:** You can also choose to back up your data to your own on-premises storage infrastructure, giving you more control over your data retention policies.

Choosing a Backup Solution:

- Consider factors like the type of data you need to back up, desired recovery time objectives (RTOs) and recovery point objectives (RPOs), and your budget.

- Look for solutions that offer features like automated backups, encryption, and easy recovery processes.

Recovery Process:

- The specific recovery process will depend on the backup solution you choose.

- Generally, it should allow you to easily restore individual files, emails, folders, or even entire user accounts.

Additional Tips:

- **Test your backups regularly:** Ensure your backups can be restored successfully when needed.

- **User Training:** Educate users about the importance of data protection and best practices to avoid accidental deletion.

By implementing a robust backup and data recovery strategy alongside Microsoft 365's built-in features, you can ensure your organization's data is protected and readily recoverable in case of unforeseen circumstances.

7.4 Customizing Office 365 for Your Needs

Here are some ways you can customize Office 365 to fit your specific needs and preferences:

Interface Customization:

- **Themes:** Change the overall look and feel of your Office 365 applications by choosing a different theme from the settings menu. Some applications may also allow you to set custom backgrounds.

- **Quick Access Toolbar:** Personalize the Quick Access Toolbar in each application with frequently used commands for easy access. Add or remove buttons based on your workflow.

- **Keyboard Shortcuts:** Utilize keyboard shortcuts to expedite actions and improve your efficiency. Many common functions have default shortcuts, and you can also customize shortcuts for specific actions you perform frequently.

Application Settings:

- **AutoSave:** Configure AutoSave settings to automatically save your work at regular intervals, preventing data loss in case of unexpected application closures.

- **Mail Options:** Fine-tune your email experience in Outlook by customizing notification settings, configuring message formatting preferences, and setting up automatic replies or forwarding rules.

- **Language and Region:** Choose the language and region settings that best suit your needs. This can affect things like date and time formats, currency symbols, and proofing tools.

Accessibility Features:

- **Explore the accessibility features built into Office 365 applications.** These features can be helpful for users with visual impairments, learning disabilities, or other needs. Features include text-to-speech conversion, Immersive Reader for improved focus while reading, and dictation for composing documents by voice.

Add-Ins and Extensions:

- The Microsoft 365 App Store offers a variety of add-ins and extensions that can extend the functionalities of the applications. Explore the store to find add-ins that cater to your specific workflows or industry needs. Some add-ins may be free, while others require a paid subscription.

Customizing Your SharePoint and OneDrive Experience:

- **Views and Layouts:** Create custom views and layouts for your document libraries in SharePoint and OneDrive to organize and categorize your files in a way that works best for you and your team.

- **Alerts:** Set up custom alerts to receive notifications when specific files or folders are modified or shared.

- **Sharing Permissions:** Manage sharing permissions for your OneDrive and SharePoint files and folders to control who can access and edit your documents.

Leveraging Microsoft Teams:

- **Teams Customization:** Create custom tabs and channels within Microsoft Teams to organize communication and collaboration around specific projects or departments.

- **Guest Access:** Enable guest access in Teams to collaborate with people outside your organization.

Admin Controls (if applicable):

- If you're an administrator for your organization's Microsoft 365 subscription, you can leverage the admin centre to manage user accounts, assign licenses, control access to features, and configure security settings to align with your organization's policies.

By implementing these customization options, you can create a more user-friendly and efficient Office 365 experience that caters to your individual work style and preferences. Explore the different settings and functionalities within each application to tailor them to your specific needs.

CHAPTER EIGHT
Case Studies and Usr Cases

8.1 Office 365 in Education

Microsoft Office 365, now known as Microsoft 365, offers a comprehensive suite of tools specifically designed to enhance learning experiences for both students and educators.

Here's a breakdown of the key benefits and functionalities:

- **Improved Collaboration:** Microsoft 365 fosters collaboration among students and teachers. Tools like Word, Excel, and PowerPoint allow for real-time co-authoring on documents and presentations, promoting teamwork and interactive learning.

- **Enhanced Communication:** Exchange Online provides students and teachers with reliable email and calendaring tools to improve communication and streamline scheduling within classrooms and school communities.

- **Accessibility and Flexibility:** Microsoft 365 offers cloud-based access to applications and storage. This allows students and teachers to work on assignments and access learning materials from anywhere with an internet connection, promoting flexible learning environments.

- **Fostering Creativity and Engagement:** Tools like Sway (a digital storytelling platform) and OneNote (a digital note-taking app) allow students to express themselves creatively and organize information effectively.

- **Streamlined Classroom Management:** Microsoft Teams acts as a central hub for creating online classrooms, facilitating discussions, sharing resources, and conducting video conferencing. This fosters a more interactive and engaging learning environment.

- **Accessibility Tools for Inclusive Learning:** Microsoft 365 offers built-in accessibility features like text-to-speech, Immersive Reader, and Learning Tools to support students with different learning styles and abilities.

Benefits for Educators:

- **Simplified Lesson Planning and Delivery:** Microsoft 365 provides tools for creating interactive lesson plans, presentations, and quizzes, saving educators valuable time and effort.

- **Automated Grading and Feedback:** Features like Forms and Stream can simplify online assessments and provide students with instant feedback.

- **Improved Communication with Parents:** Microsoft 365 facilitates communication between teachers and parents through email or collaboration tools like Teams.

- **Professional Development and Collaboration:** The platform allows educators to connect with colleagues, share best practices, and participate in professional development opportunities.

Deployment Options and Affordability:

- Microsoft offers various subscription plans for educational institutions, often at significantly discounted rates compared to commercial licenses. These plans cater to different needs and budgets.

- Some schools may even qualify for free access to the basic functionalities of Microsoft 365 tools.

Overall, Microsoft 365 in Education empowers a more collaborative, engaging, and accessible learning experience for students and educators alike.

Here are some additional resources you might find helpful:

- **Microsoft Education Website:** This website provides comprehensive information about Microsoft 365 Education, including features, benefits, and getting started guides.

8.2 Office 365 for Small Businesses

Here's a breakdown of how Microsoft 365 (formerly Office 365) can be a valuable asset for small businesses:

Enhanced Productivity and Collaboration:

- **Essential applications:** Get access to the familiar Microsoft Office suite (Word, Excel, PowerPoint, Outlook) for creating professional documents, presentations, spreadsheets, and managing email effectively.

- **Real-time co-authoring:** Collaborate on documents and presentations with colleagues simultaneously, streamlining workflows and boosting productivity.

- **Improved communication:** Microsoft Teams provides a central hub for instant messaging, video conferencing, file sharing, and project management, fostering better communication and teamwork within your small business.

Increased Mobility and Flexibility:

- **Cloud-based access:** Access applications, documents, and email from anywhere, on any device (PC, Mac, phone, tablet) with an internet connection. This empowers employees to work remotely or flexibly, improving work-life balance and overall satisfaction.

- **Offline functionality:** Work on documents even without an internet connection (with limitations) and have them automatically sync when you go back online.

Enhanced Security and Manageability:

- **Centralized administration:** Manage user accounts, assign licenses, and control access to applications and data from a single, web-based admin centre.

- **Robust security features:** Benefit from enterprise-grade security features like data encryption, spam and malware filtering, and multi-factor authentication to protect your business from cyber threats.

- **Automatic updates:** Stay updated with the latest features and security patches without manual intervention, ensuring you have the most secure and up-to-date applications.

Cost-Effectiveness:

- **Subscription-based model:** Pay a predictable monthly or annual subscription fee per user, eliminating the need for upfront software purchases. This can be easier to budget for a small business.

- **Scalability:** Easily add or remove users as your business grows, ensuring you only pay for what you need.

Additional Considerations:

- **Choose the right plan:** Microsoft 365 offers various plans with different features and storage capacities. Carefully evaluate your needs and choose a plan that best suits your business size and budget.

- **System requirements:** Ensure your devices meet the minimum system requirements for smooth operation of Microsoft 365 applications.

- **Learning curve:** There might be a slight learning curve for some users who are not familiar with the latest features of Microsoft Office applications.

Overall, Microsoft 365 offers a compelling suite of tools and features designed to empower small businesses to collaborate effectively, improve productivity, work flexibly, and stay secure in today's digital landscape.

8.3 Enterprise Solutions with Office 365

Microsoft 365 goes beyond the familiar productivity applications for businesses of all sizes, offering robust enterprise solutions that cater to the needs of large organizations with complex workflows and demanding requirements. Here's a closer look at some key features that make Microsoft 365 a powerful tool for enterprises:

Enhanced Security and Compliance:

- **Advanced Threat Protection:** Safeguard your organization from sophisticated cyber threats with features like real-time malware detection, email phishing protection, and data loss prevention.

- **Data Governance and Compliance:** Ensure adherence to industry regulations and internal data governance policies with tools for data classification, information rights management, and eDiscovery.

- **Multi-Geo Capabilities:** For organizations with international operations, manage data residency requirements by storing data in specific geographic locations.

Improved Productivity and Collaboration:

- **Power Platform:** Empower citizen developers to create custom business applications, automate workflows, and extend the functionalities of Microsoft 365 to meet specific needs of your organization.

- **Streamlined Communication:** Microsoft Teams offers advanced features for large teams, such as live captions and translation, breakout rooms for focused discussions, and improved meeting management functionalities.

- **Enterprise Voice and Video Calling:** Make and receive high-quality voice and video calls directly within Teams, eliminating the need for separate phone systems and simplifying communication channels.

Advanced Analytics and Business Intelligence:

- **Power BI:** Gain valuable insights from your data with Power BI, a robust business intelligence tool for data visualization, interactive reports, and self-service analytics.

- **Microsoft Flow:** Automate complex workflows by connecting various Microsoft 365 services and third-party applications, streamlining data flow and eliminating manual tasks.

- **Customizable Dashboards:** Create personalized dashboards to monitor key performance indicators (KPIs), track project progress, and gain real-time insights into your organization's health.

Additional Benefits:

- **Scalability and Flexibility:** Microsoft 365 scales to accommodate the growing needs of large organizations. Easily add or remove users, adjust storage quotas, and activate new services as needed.

- **Centralized Management:** Manage user accounts, licenses, security settings, and all Microsoft 365 services from a single, web-based admin centre.
- **Deployment Options:** Choose between cloud-based, on-premises, or a hybrid deployment model to suit your organization's specific infrastructure and security requirements.

Exploring Enterprise Plans:

Microsoft 365 offers various enterprise plans, including:

- **Microsoft 365 E3:** Provides core security and compliance features, collaboration tools, and the Power Platform for building custom applications.
- **Microsoft 365 E5:** Includes all the functionalities of E3 with additional advanced analytics, voice capabilities, and enhanced security features.

By carefully evaluating your organization's needs and choosing the right plan, Microsoft 365 can become a powerful enterprise solution that empowers your workforce, streamlines workflows, strengthens security, and ultimately helps your business thrive in the competitive digital landscape.

8.4 Non-Profit Organizations and Office 365

Non-profit organizations often juggle limited resources with a vast amount of work. Microsoft 365 can be a valuable asset in this context, offering a suite of productivity and collaboration tools at a significantly discounted rate or even free of charge. Here's how Microsoft 365 can benefit non-profits:

Enhanced Collaboration and Communication:

- **Improved Teamwork:** Microsoft 365 applications like Word, Excel, PowerPoint, and OneNote enable teams to work together on documents, presentations, and spreadsheets in real-time, fostering better collaboration and project management.
- **Streamlined Communication:** Microsoft Teams provides a central hub for instant messaging, video conferencing, file sharing, and project management. This keeps teams connected and allows for efficient communication, even for geographically dispersed teams.
- **Effective Fundraising and Donor Management:** Use applications like Excel and Access to manage donor data, track fundraising campaigns, and create reports for better organization and outreach.

Increased Efficiency and Productivity:

- **Cloud-Based Accessibility:** Access files, email, and applications from anywhere, on any device with an internet connection. This empowers staff and volunteers to work remotely or flexibly, improving productivity and streamlining workflows.

- **Automated Workflows:** Microsoft Power Automate (formerly Flow) can automate repetitive tasks, saving time and allowing staff to focus on higher-value activities. For example, automate sending welcome emails to new donors or generating reports.

- **Improved Organization and Knowledge Sharing:** Use SharePoint Online to create central repositories for storing and sharing documents, resources, and best practices across the organization.

Cost-Effectiveness and Scalability:

- **Discounted Subscriptions:** Microsoft offers significant discounts or even free subscriptions to eligible non-profit organizations, making Microsoft 365 a budget-friendly solution.

- **Scalability:** As your non-profit grows, you can easily add or remove users from your subscription plan, ensuring you only pay for what you need.

Security and Compliance:

- **Robust Security Features:** Benefit from enterprise-grade security features like data encryption, spam and malware filtering, and multi-factor authentication to protect your organization's sensitive data.

- **Compliance Tools:** Some plans offer features to help with regulatory compliance, such as data loss prevention and eDiscovery.

Getting Started with Microsoft 365 for Non-Profits:

- **Verify Eligibility:** Check if your organization qualifies for the non-profit licensing program through Microsoft or its authorized partners like TechSoup.

- **Choose the Right Plan:** Microsoft offers various plans with different features and storage capacities. Evaluate your needs and choose a plan that best suits your organization.

- **Training and Support:** Microsoft and its partners offer resources and training materials to help non-profits get the most out of Microsoft 365.

Overall, Microsoft 365 can be a game-changer for non-profit organizations, empowering staff and volunteers to collaborate more effectively, work efficiently, and achieve your mission-driven goals.

CHAPTER NINE
Future of Office 365

9.1 Upcoming Features and Updates

Since Microsoft 365 is a cloud-based service, they are constantly rolling out updates and adding new features. While there isn't one definitive source to track every upcoming change, here are some ways to stay informed:

- **Microsoft 365 Roadmap:** This is the official Microsoft resource that provides a high-level view of features currently in development, planned for future releases, and recently released. You can browse the roadmap by category (e.g., Teams, Excel, Security) or search for specific features you're interested in.

- **Microsoft 365 Blog:** This blog keeps you updated on the latest announcements, new features, and upcoming changes for Microsoft 365. They often publish articles in conjunction with roadmap updates, providing more detailed explanations about new features.

- **Microsoft Tech Community:** This online forum allows you to connect with other Microsoft 365 users and administrators. Community members often share insights and discuss upcoming features based on rumours, leaks, or early access experiences. Keep in mind that information here may not be official from Microsoft.

- **Tech News Websites:** Reputable technology news websites like The Verge, ZDNet, or PC Magazine often cover upcoming Microsoft 365 features based on press releases, conferences, or insider leaks.

By following these resources, you can stay ahead of the curve and learn about exciting new features that can potentially improve your productivity and collaboration using Microsoft 365.

9.2 Trends in Cloud Computing and Collaboration

The landscape of cloud computing and collaboration is constantly evolving, with new trends emerging all the time. Here's a look at some of the most prominent trends you can expect to see in the coming years:

1. Continued Rise of Hybrid and Multi-Cloud Environments:

- Businesses are increasingly moving towards a hybrid or multi-cloud strategy, using a combination of public cloud services, private clouds, and on-premises infrastructure. This allows them to leverage the benefits of each platform (scalability, cost-effectiveness, security) for different workloads.

2. Growing Importance of Artificial Intelligence (AI) and Machine Learning (ML):

- AI and ML are being integrated into cloud services to automate tasks, improve efficiency, and deliver more personalized user experiences. For example, AI can be used to optimize resource allocation, automate data backup and recovery, and even enhance collaboration tools with features like smart suggestions and content translation.

3. Edge Computing Takes Centre Stage:

- Edge computing brings processing power and data storage closer to where data is generated (e.g., factory machines, sensors). This reduces latency, improves performance for real-time applications, and alleviates bandwidth limitations for cloud communication. Collaboration tools integrated with edge computing can enable faster decision-making and real-time data analysis within teams.

4. Increased Focus on Security and Compliance:

- Cloud security remains a top concern. As businesses move more data and operations to the cloud, robust security measures are crucial. Expect to see advancements in cloud security solutions like data encryption, multi-factor authentication, and threat detection features. Additionally, compliance with data privacy regulations will continue to be a major consideration for cloud adoption.

5. The Rise of Low-Code/No-Code Development:

- Low-code/no-code platforms allow users with minimal coding experience to build cloud applications. This trend empowers businesses to create custom collaboration tools and workflows that cater to their specific needs without relying heavily on IT departments.

6. The Future of Work and Collaboration:

- As remote and hybrid work models become more mainstream, collaboration tools will continue to evolve to support geographically dispersed teams. Features like real-time co-authoring, integrated video conferencing, and advanced team communication functionalities will be even more critical.

7. Integration with the Internet of Things (IoT):

- As more devices become connected to the internet (IoT), cloud platforms will play a central role in managing and analysing data collected from these devices. Collaboration tools can leverage this data to improve workflow automation and decision-making within organizations.

8. Growing Emphasis on Sustainability:

- Cloud providers are increasingly focusing on sustainable practices and energy-efficient data centres. Businesses will be looking for cloud solutions that align with their environmental sustainability goals.

By staying informed about these trends, you can make informed decisions about cloud-based collaboration tools and strategies that can empower your teams and optimize your organization's productivity in the ever-changing digital landscape.

9.3 Office 365 and Artificial Intelligence

AI-powered Features

- **Intelligent Search:** Utilizes AI algorithms to provide relevant search results across Office 365 applications.

- **Ideas in Excel:** Uses AI to analyse data patterns and suggest insights and visualizations in Excel.

- **Designer in PowerPoint:** AI-driven tool that suggests design ideas for PowerPoint presentations.

- **MyAnalytics:** AI-powered personal productivity insights that help users understand work habits and improve efficiency.

Microsoft Graph

- **Data Connectivity:** Utilizes AI to connect and analyse data across Office 365 applications, providing personalized experiences.

- **Recommendations:** Offers personalized recommendations based on user behaviour and preferences.

Cognitive Services Integration

- **Text Analysis:** Allows users to analyse and extract insights from text data within Office 365 applications.

- **Speech Recognition:** Enables voice commands and dictation within Office applications using AI-driven speech recognition technology.

Language Translation

- **Translator for Word:** AI-powered tool that provides real-time translation of text in Word documents.

- **Translator for Outlook:** Integrates with Outlook to translate emails and messages into multiple languages.

Outlook Features

- **Focused Inbox:** AI-driven feature that prioritizes important emails based on user interactions.

- **Email Insights:** Provides insights and suggestions to improve email communication efficiency.

Security and Compliance

- **Threat Intelligence:** Utilizes AI to analyse and detect potential security threats across Office 365 applications.

- **Data Loss Prevention:** AI-driven feature that helps prevent the accidental sharing of sensitive information.

Future Developments

- **Continued Innovation:** Microsoft continues to invest in AI research and development to enhance Office 365 with new AI-driven features and capabilities.

- **Integration with Other AI Platforms:** Collaboration with other AI platforms and technologies to further enhance Office 365's AI capabilities.

By leveraging artificial intelligence, Office 365 offers a range of intelligent features and capabilities that improve productivity, enhance collaboration, and ensure security and compliance across the platform.

CHAPTER TEN
Appendices

10.1 Keyboard Shortcuts

Here are some essential keyboard shortcuts for Microsoft Office 365 applications to help boost your productivity:

General Office Shortcuts

- Ctrl + N: Create a new document, workbook, or presentation
- Ctrl + O: Open an existing file
- Ctrl + S: Save the current file
- Ctrl + P: Print the current file
- Ctrl + Z: Undo the last action
- Ctrl + Y: Redo the last undone action
- Ctrl + F: Find text or other content
- Ctrl + H: Find and replace text or other content

Microsoft Word

- Ctrl + B: Bold selected text
- Ctrl + I: Italicize selected text
- Ctrl + U: Underline selected text
- Ctrl + A: Select all content in the document
- Ctrl + C: Copy selected text or content
- Ctrl + V: Paste copied text or content
- Ctrl + X: Cut selected text or content
- Ctrl + K: Insert a hyperlink
- Ctrl + Enter: Insert a page break

Microsoft Excel

- Ctrl + Shift + L: Toggle filters
- Ctrl + T: Create a table
- Ctrl + Arrow Key: Move to the edge of the data region

- Ctrl + Space: Select entire column

- Shift + Space: Select entire row

- F2: Edit the active cell

- Alt + Enter: Start a new line within a cell

- Ctrl + D: Fill down

- Ctrl + R: Fill right

Microsoft PowerPoint

- Ctrl + M: Insert a new slide

- Ctrl + D: Duplicate the selected slide

- Ctrl + Shift + Up/Down Arrow: Move the selected slide up or down

- F5: Start the slideshow from the beginning

- Shift + F5: Start the slideshow from the current slide

- Ctrl + K: Insert a hyperlink

- Alt + Shift + Left/Right Arrow: Promote or demote a bullet point

Microsoft Outlook

- Ctrl + R: Reply to the selected email

- Ctrl + Shift + R: Reply all to the selected email

- Ctrl + F: Forward the selected email

- Ctrl + N: Create a new email

- Ctrl + Shift + M: Open a new email message

- Ctrl + 1: Switch to Mail view

- Ctrl + 2: Switch to Calendar view

- Ctrl + 3: Switch to Contacts view

- Ctrl + Enter: Send the current email

Microsoft OneNote

- Ctrl + N: Create a new page

- Ctrl + T: Create a new section

- Ctrl + Alt + D: Dock OneNote to the desktop

- Ctrl + 1: Apply or remove a to-do tag
- Ctrl + Shift + Alt + N: Create a new subpage
- Alt + Shift + Up/Down Arrow: Move the current page up or down in the section
- Ctrl + Shift + G: Open the current notebook

Microsoft Teams

- Ctrl + N: Start a new chat
- Ctrl + E: Go to the search bar
- Ctrl + 1: Go to Activity feed
- Ctrl + 2: Go to Chat
- Ctrl + 3: Go to Teams
- Ctrl + Shift + M: Mute/unmute your microphone
- Ctrl + Shift + O: Turn on/off your camera
- Ctrl + Space: Push to talk

These shortcuts will help you navigate and operate efficiently across the various Office 365 applications.

10.2 Glossary of Terms

Active Directory (AD): A directory service developed by Microsoft for Windows domain networks. It manages permissions and access to networked resources.

Cloud Computing: The delivery of computing services over the internet, including storage, processing, and software applications.

Collaboration Tools: Software and technologies that allow multiple users to work together on documents, projects, or tasks in real time or asynchronously.

Exchange Online: A hosted messaging solution that delivers email, calendar, contacts, and tasks. It runs on Microsoft Exchange Server.

Lync (Now Microsoft Teams): A unified communications platform that integrates with Office 365. It includes instant messaging, video conferencing, and voice calling.

Microsoft 365 (Formerly Office 365): A subscription service that includes access to Office applications and other productivity services enabled over the internet (cloud services).

Office Web Apps: Web-based versions of Microsoft Office applications such as Word, Excel, PowerPoint, and OneNote, accessible through a web browser.

OneDrive: Microsoft's cloud storage service that allows users to store files and access them from any device with an internet connection.

SharePoint Online: A cloud-based service that helps organizations share and manage content, knowledge, and applications to empower teamwork.

Single Sign-On (SSO): An authentication process that allows a user to access multiple applications with one set of login credentials.

Subscription Plan: A pricing model where users pay a recurring fee at regular intervals (monthly or annually) to access software and services.

Teams: Microsoft's platform for teamwork that integrates people, content, and tools. It includes chat, meetings, file collaboration, and application integration.

Two-Factor Authentication (2FA): An additional layer of security that requires not only a password and username but also something that only the user has on them, such as a mobile device.

Virtual Office: A working environment that is not based in any one physical location, but rather uses technology to enable employees to work from various locations.

Windows Live ID (Now Microsoft Account): A single sign-on web service provided by Microsoft that allows users to log into many websites using a single set of credentials.

Yammer: An enterprise social networking service used for private communication within organizations, included with Office 365 subscriptions.

10.3 Additional Resources and Reading

In addition to the information we've covered, here are some excellent resources for further reading on Microsoft 365:

Official Microsoft Documentation:

- Microsoft 365 for admins: This is the official starting point for learning how to manage your Microsoft 365 tenant. It includes comprehensive guides, tutorials, and step-by-step instructions for various tasks.

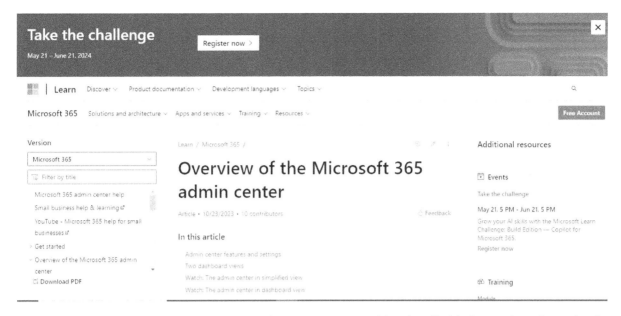

- Microsoft 365 Service Descriptions: This resource provides detailed information about the features and functionalities included in each Microsoft 365 subscription plan.

News and Updates:

- Microsoft 365 Blog: Stay up-to-date on the latest announcements, new features, and upcoming changes for Microsoft 365.

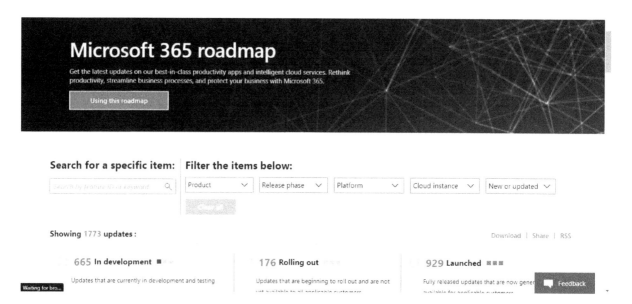

- Microsoft Tech Community: Engage with other Microsoft 365 users and administrators, ask questions, and find solutions to common challenges.

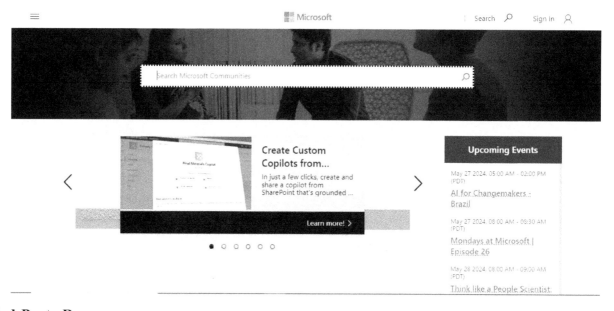

Third-Party Resources:

- PC Magazine offers reviews, comparisons, and helpful articles on getting the most out of Microsoft 365.

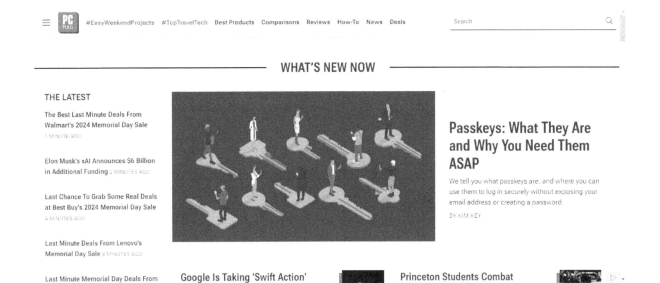

- This series by Wiley provides a user-friendly introduction to Microsoft 365 applications and features.

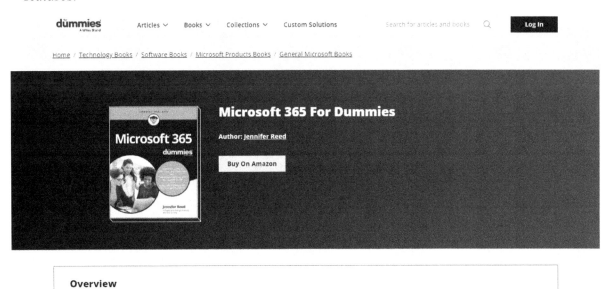

- Search YouTube for tutorials, demonstrations, and video guides on using various Microsoft 365 applications.

Training and Certification:

- Microsoft 365 Learning Paths: Microsoft offers a variety of learning paths and certifications to help you develop your expertise in Microsoft 365 administration.

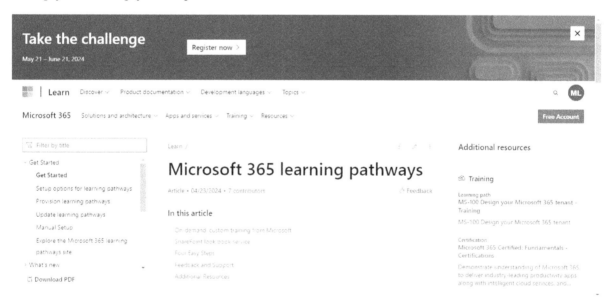

I hope this helps! If you have any specific areas of interest within Microsoft 365, let me know and I can try to find some more tailored resources for you.